IDLEN

C000185997

"*Idleness* nails the myth that any
or poorly paid – is better than n‹
case that empowering workers and improving the quality of
work can help drive productivity and sustainable growth."

PAUL NOWAK, General Secretary-designate, TUC

"The question of how to help women escape poverty pay has
long been with us, but finding the answer has never been more
important. This book is a crucial intervention on a subject
that deserves to be right at the top of our agenda."

HARRIET HARMAN, MP

"An engaging and insightful read that artfully reflects on the Giant
of 'Idleness' in a contemporary context. Jones and Kumar challenge
the prevailing economic orthodoxy on work and employment,
arguing that economic policy needs to be more relevant. If we are
to address the UK's ailing economic performance and productivity
they highlight the need to empower employees and improve
management practice, and only then will we realize the benefits."

PROFESSOR TIM VORLEY, Pro Vice-Chancellor and
Dean, Oxford Brookes Business School

"An authoritative account of how the UK labour market really
works, *Idleness* is full of important insights, and more than a few
home truths about the failures of public policy. Jones and Kumar
challenge the orthodoxy that low pay and job insecurity results
from poor productivity growth, and instead make the case for
empowering workers as part of a new economic model for the UK."

CRAIG BERRY, Head of Policy, Institute for Innovation and
Public Purpose, University College London

FIVE GIANTS: A NEW BEVERIDGE REPORT

Consultant editor: Danny Dorling, *University of Oxford*

In November 1942, William Beveridge published *Social Insurance and Allied Services*, the result of a survey work commissioned the year before by the wartime coalition government. In what soon became known as simply "The Beveridge Report", five impediments to social progress were identified: the giants of Want, Disease, Squalor, Ignorance and Idleness. Tackling these giants was to be at the heart of postwar reconstruction. The welfare state, including national insurance, child allowances and the National Health Service, was a direct result of Beveridge's recommendations.

To mark the eightieth anniversary of the Report's publication, the authors in this series consider the progress made against Beveridge's giants, and whether they have diminished or risen up to again stalk the land. They also reflect on how the fight against poverty, unfit housing, ill-health, unemployment and poor education could be renewed as the countries of the UK emerge from a series of deeply damaging, divisive and impoverishing crises.

As an establishment figure, a Liberal and a eugenicist, Beveridge was an unlikely coordinator of the radical changes that improved so many peoples' lives. However, the banking crisis at the end of the 1920s, the mass unemployment and impoverishment of the 1930s, and the economic shock of the Second World War changed what was possible to what became essential. Old certainties were swept aside as much from within the existing order as from outside it.

The books explore the topic without constraint and the results are informative, entertaining and concerning. They aim to ignite a broader debate about the future of our society and encourage the vision and aspiration that previous generations held for us.

Want by Helen Barnard

Disease by Frances Darlington-Pollock

Squalor by Daniel Renwick and Robbie Shilliam

Ignorance by Sally Tomlinson

Idleness by Katy Jones and Ashwin Kumar

IDLENESS

Katy Jones and Ashwin Kumar

agenda
publishing

First published in 2022 by Agenda Publishing

Agenda Publishing Limited
The Core
Bath Lane
Newcastle Helix
Newcastle upon Tyne
NE4 5TF

www.agendapub.com

ISBN 978-1-78821-454-4
ISBN 978-1-78821-455-1 (ePDF)
ISBN 978-1-78821-456-8 (ePUB)

British Library Cataloguing-in-Publication Data
A catalogue record for this book is available
from the British Library

Typeset in Nocturne by Patty Rennie

Printed and bound in the UK by CPI Group (UK) Ltd,
Croydon, CR0 4YY

Contents

Preface

Before the start of the Second World War, the UK had experienced two decades of high unemployment. For Beveridge writing in 1942, the Giant of "Idleness" was primarily about worklessness and a lack of jobs for the male breadwinner. Today's labour market is very different. Far fewer people are unemployed, the number of women in paid work has increased dramatically, but in-work poverty is rising and increasing numbers of people face new forms of insecurity in work. Today's problem is not a lack of work, but a lack of quality work with a good level of pay.

Although the mantra that "work is the best way out of poverty" remains firmly entrenched in parts of the political psyche, the reality is that the UK has become stuck in a low-pay low-productivity rut. Rising in-work poverty, low productivity levels, falling rates of progression and increasing "precaritization" of the workforce increasingly call this into question. Tackling un- and underemployment in a post-Brexit, post-pandemic UK necessitates a substantial shift in our understanding of the problem and our response to it. This is crucial if ambitions to "build back better" are to be realized. In this book, we show why quality of work is the most pressing labour market issue facing the UK today, and what must be done to solve it.

Underlying all of these issues is the question of power in the labour market. In the past, this discussion has focused on union-ization and collective bargaining, which undoubtedly improves outcomes for workers. But there is a more subtle way in which worker power needs to be considered. By and large, for people who are unemployed or on a low income, power is in short supply. The way the state engages with people out of work, through coercive active labour market policies, a lack of concern for skills and career progression and a one-size-fits-all approach to out-of-work support that ignores the needs of lone parents, disabled people and others, exacerbates this problem.

The degradation of social infrastructure – declining local bus services, childcare services that don't meet the shift patterns of low-paid workers – conspire to create barriers to work, especially for women. If you need to be at the school gate by 3.15pm, the pool of potential jobs shrinks very quickly. As we show, childcare and transport are not only social policy issues but fundamental to tackling low-pay low-productivity Britain.

The dominant policy thinking about regulation of the labour market presupposes a trade-off between fairness and efficiency: yes, we can protect working conditions but only at the expense of our economic health. In fact, as we show, this contributes to the imbalance of power between workers and employers and to the low-pay low-productivity equilibrium that locks too many people into low-paid work, and slows down the UK's economic performance.

The UK needs a fresh new vision that empowers work-ers, rather than making them subservient to a low-pay, low productivity economy. One that shifts us away from positioning unemployment and low pay as a "behavioural problem" towards an approach that opens up, rather than creates barriers to quality opportunities for all. In the spirit of the Beveridge Report, we hope this book makes a start.

Thanks to Ellen Boeren, Hayley Bennett, Lisa Scullion and Dave Innes for providing invaluable feedback on early chapters; to

Alison Howson, our editor at Agenda Publishing, for her patience and guidance; and to Ally, Riya and Joel for their support and encouragement throughout.

1

A changing labour market: from Beveridge to Brexit

"The welfare system ... has created ghettos of workless-ness where generations have grown up without hope or aspiration ... the benefits system has created pockets of worklessness across the country where idleness is insti-tutionalized ... I want to transform the system so that we can once again tackle this growing problem that Beveridge identified and we must slay."

Iain Duncan Smith, Secretary of
State for Work and Pensions, 2010

Today's labour market is very different to the one in which the Beveridge Report was conceived. Commissioned in 1941 at the height of the Second World War, it was written as part of the efforts of the wartime government to "plan the peace" but drew on prewar experiences. Almost the entirety of the 1920s and 1930s had seen very high rates of unemployment in the UK. The years after the First World War saw a prolonged slump that was exacerbated by the fallout from the Wall Street Crash of 1929.

As shown in Figure 1.1, it was only at the very end of the 1930s, shortly before the onset of the Second World War, that unemployment had returned to more typical levels. Beveridge addressed, therefore, what the government should do to support those looking for work – to avoid "Want" – and what the government could do to help people back into work – to avoid "Idleness".

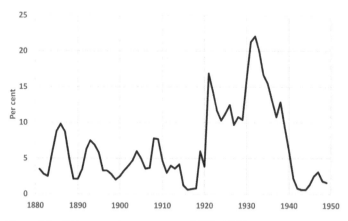

Figure 1.1   UK unemployment rate, 1881–1951

Source: Denman & MacDonald (1996).

These questions are still part of our policy conversation today, but perhaps with insufficient recognition of how the UK labour market has changed over the past few decades. Contrary to the comments of Iain Duncan Smith that opened this chapter, the UK is not facing a situation in which "idleness is institutionalized". In fact, we have the highest employment rates ever seen and the key issue facing the UK is that too many people are trapped in low-paid insecure work.

It is important, therefore, to start with a clear idea of what has actually happened in the UK labour market over the past few decades and how much has changed since Beveridge's time.

First and foremost, recent years have seen historically high levels of employment. Figure 1.2 shows that, before the pandemic, January 2020 saw the highest proportion of people in work ever recorded. Even in the depths of the Covid-19 recession, the employment rate was higher than ever seen before 2016.

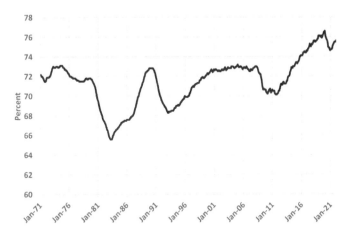

Figure 1.2   UK employment rate, 1971–2021

Source: ONS, time series LF24.

Arguably, the recent highs in employment rates, and success in preventing recession-related worklessness, have followed trends seen for two decades. In terms of economic activity, the 2008 recession was the most severe that the UK had seen in peacetime since the 1930s.[1] Yet the drop in employment was significantly less than in the 1980s or 1990s recessions. The Covid recession of 2020 was even more severe, and yet the furlough scheme – although not perfect – kept huge numbers of people in employment. So, we have many more people in work and recent

---

1 The drop in quarterly real GDP per head (ONS series IHXW) from the pre-recession peak was 6.9 per cent in 2009 Q3; this compares to 2.7 per cent in 1992 Q2; 5.5 per cent in 1981 Q1; and 5.4 per cent in 1975 Q3. The drop from the pre-pandemic peak in 2020 Q2 was 22 per cent.

experience suggests we're better at keeping people in work when the economy slumps than in the past.

The gender structure of work has changed dramatically during the twentieth century. Analysis of census data by Gales and Marks (1974) shows that, whilst employment rates for single women were relatively similar to today, only around one in ten married women were in or looking for paid work prior to the Second World War. This increased to a quarter by 1951[2] and half by 1971. The increase in women's employment has continued in subsequent decades and, as Figure 1.3 shows, at 72 per cent, the rate is now only a few percentage points behind the male employment rate.

There are three drivers of the increase in women's employment. The first is the reduction in the extent to which marriage itself was a reason for women to leave the labour market. For example, the BBC and the "home" civil service prohibited married women working for them until 1944 and 1946 respectively (Iglikowski 2015), and the Foreign Office persisted with this rule until 1973 (McCarthy 2014).[3] Secondly, the age at which first children are born has been getting steadily later. The proportion of 25-year-old women in 2000 who had had at least one child was half that of women 30 years previously. Finally, fewer women leave the labour market on the birth of their first child and in the following years: two out of five women born in 1958 were still working two years after their first child was born.

---

2 Gales and Marks (1974) note that this may be an underestimate because the instructions on how to record part-time work in the census changed over time. For example, for the 1951 census, women who were spending most of their time looking after the home were to be classified as "unoccupied" and so women in paid work for small numbers of hours each week may have been missed from employment totals.

3 Foreign and Commonwealth Office (2018) describes the marriage bar as being "rescinded" in 1972, but other sources say 1973, which may reflect the difference between the decision being taken and implemented.

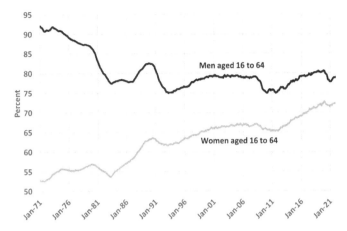

Figure 1.3   UK male and female employment rates, 1971–2021

Source: ONS, time series MGSV, LF25.

This rose to three out of five for those born in 1970 (Roantree & Vira 2018).

However, whilst the gender structure of work has changed dramatically, the gender structure of housework and childcare remains highly imbalanced (see, e.g., Wishart *et al.* 2019). The result is that much of the increase in women's employment has been in part-time work.

As more married women entered the labour market in the post-war decades, the proportion working part-time increased steadily – from 12 per cent in England and Wales in 1951 to 33 per cent in 1966 (Gales & Marks 1974). By 1984, 43 per cent of women in work in the UK worked part-time, and the rate has remained around this level for most of the period since. Thus, the early years of increasing women's employment were characterized by increases in part-time work. Since the early 1980s, the increases have been more evenly split between full- and part-time work, with slightly faster growth in full-time work. However, it is notable that, since the mid-1990s, the proportion of families with no-one in work has not fallen significantly, despite more women working. Much of the recent increase has happened among families where there was already one person working.

Despite substantial increases in employment rates since Beveridge's time, pay remains substantially lower for women. Overall, median annual pay for employees in 2021 was 31 per cent lower for women than men. Fairly obviously, working part-time will reduce weekly wages. However, even when stripping out the effects of lower working hours, median hourly pay for women was still 16 per cent lower than for men (ONS 2021a). About half of this gap is due to lower hourly pay rates amongst full-time employees.[4] The remainder arises from the fact that so many more women work part-time, where pay rates are substantially lower.[5]

The standard economists' account of wages is that they are linked to "human capital" – the skills and experience built up by individuals through education, training and work experience. However, it is clear that, for part-time workers, one part of this equation does not work. Analysis by the Joseph Rowntree Foundation (2017: 37), updated by the authors with more recent data in Figure 1.4, shows that there is little difference in median hourly pay between part-time workers with no qualifications, GCSEs, and A levels. This is in sharp contrast to full-time workers where the typical picture is seen: at each level of qualification, median pay rates rise. For people working part-time, there is virtually no return on skills for those without a degree.

These changes in the gender structure of work represent a huge structural shift since Beveridge's time. Firstly, women

---

4 The gender pay gap for full-time employees was 7.9 per cent in April 2021 (ONS 2021b).

5 Median hourly pay for full-time employees was £15.65 in April 2021 and £10.64 for part-time employees (ONS 2021a).

are much more likely to work – after marriage and after having children. However, a significant proportion of this is part-time. Working part-time has a dual effect: lower hours of work per week and lower hourly rates of pay.

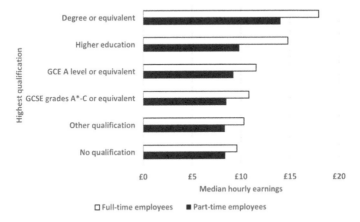

Figure 1.4   Median hourly rates of pay by qualification for full- and part-time workers, Q4 2019.

Source: Labour Force Survey, Oct–Dec 2019; based on chart in Barnard *et al.* (2017).

The lack of return on skills for part-time workers has created a two-tier workforce. There are those whose labour supply is unconstrained by caring responsibilities who, despite ongoing gender pay gaps for full-time workers, have more chance of being able to take on work that reflects their education, training and qualifications. And there are those for whom the constraints of caring means that access to work that reflects their qualifications and skills is in short supply.

IN-WORK POVERTY

"I believe in the dignity of labor, whether with head or hand; that the world owes no man a living but that it owes every man an opportunity to make a living." John D. Rockefeller, Jr

Having more people in work than ever before should be a success story. It is widely believed that work should provide a "living" – that a good day's work is sufficient to provide an adequate income. Today, that is not the case for many people. More than one in six working families are in poverty and, as Figure 1.5 shows, in-work poverty is now more common than out-of-work poverty. We may have the highest ever employment rates but we also have the highest ever rates of in-work poverty. The rise in employment has not translated into greater levels of economic well-being.[6]

Low pay is normally defined as two-thirds of median hourly earnings – i.e. with respect to hourly pay (see, e.g., Cominetti *et al*. 2021). There is a substantial overlap between low pay and poverty, but it is not a simple relationship.

As Figure 1.6 shows, there have been two periods over the past two decades in which in-work poverty has risen: 2004–08, and 2013 onwards but there is a different explanation in each case. In the first of these two periods, hourly pay at the bottom of the earnings distribution failed to keep up with the average rate of growth in the economy. As a result, people on low earnings fell behind the rest of society and in-work poverty increased (Innes 2020).

---

6 17.4 per cent of benefit units (families) with at least one person in work are in poverty – higher than at any point since 1996/97, and 57.4 per cent of families in poverty have at least one person in work (Households Below Average Income dataset 1994/95–2019/20).

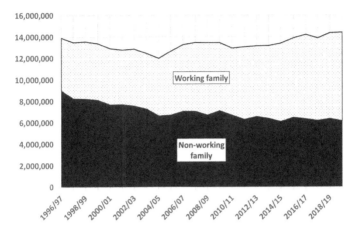

Figure 1.5   People in poverty by family work status

Source: Households Below Average Income, using the After Housing Costs measure of poverty.

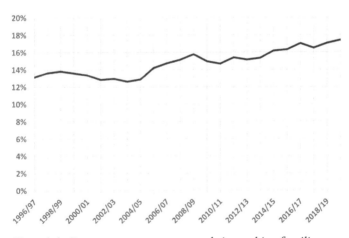

Figure 1.6   Poverty rate amongst people in working families

Source: Households Below Average Income.

However, that didn't happen in the most recent period. In fact, from 2016 onwards, faster increases in the minimum wage meant that hourly pay at the bottom of the earnings distribution rose as fast as average earnings (Innes 2020). However, for most low-income families, reductions in in-work benefits, and increases in housing costs, more than cancelled out the effects of the increases in the minimum wage.

Another factor that has been in play over the past two decades has been reductions in working hours. As Innes (2020) notes, average hours per worker have fallen since 2000 by more for lower income families than others.

The situation today is that receiving a low hourly rate of pay and working part-time are both an important part of the story of in-work poverty. There are lots of families with part-time workers and people on low hourly rates of pay who are not in poverty, perhaps because they live with a higher earner. But most families in in-work poverty either have someone working part-time, or on low pay.

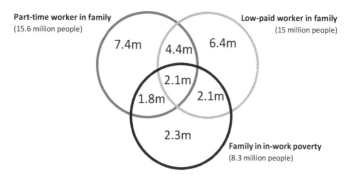

Figure 1.7   Combinations of low pay, part-time work and in-work poverty amongst people in UK working families, 2019/20

Source: Family Resources Survey and Households Below Average Income, 2019/20.

INSECURITY

Clearly the UK labour market has changed considerably over the past few decades. However, there is one area in which we have returned to some of the conditions of Beveridge's time. Whereas insecurity in the labour market was common in the early part of the twentieth century, we saw progressive improvement in working conditions in the latter part of the century. However, the past decade has seen increasing insecurity driven by both technological and legal innovation. Technology now exists to pay workers by the minute. Legal innovations have developed to undermine the employment protections developed over many decades.

There are currently around one million people whose work is governed by zero-hours contracts (ONS 2021c: table 1) – arrangements where workers are not told of the hours they are to work until the employer decides, which may be as little as two weeks beforehand, and sometimes even less (Incomes Data Research 2018). The Chartered Institute of Personnel and Development (CIPD) estimates that there are a further 400,000 people on short-hours contracts (CIPD 2015), which guarantee between one and eight hours of work and, similarly, depend on employer notification for any more hours (Recruiting Times 2017).

According to the CIPD, zero-hours contracts work well for many people who are on them, but not for everybody. Roughly one in five of people on zero-hours contracts are in full-time education (ONS 2021c: table 11) and average job satisfaction levels are similar to those for all employees. However, more than a quarter of people on these contracts want more hours of work (ONS 2021c: table 14), and among those who do, satisfaction levels are much lower (CIPD 2015: 32).

The theory of zero-hours and short-hours contracts is that they offer welcome flexibility for people (such as full-time students) who need it and enable employers to manage short-term fluctuations in demand. However, there is ample evidence of a mismatch between theory and practice. For example, around half of people on zero-hours contracts have been with their employer for at least two years (ONS 2021c: table 13) and many use them to cover the same shifts on a regular basis (Maguire 2019).

The Contracts of Employment Act 1963 is sometimes considered the first piece of modern employment protection legislation in the UK, offering a right to written specification of hours of work, pay rates, and notice periods (Grunfeld 1964). Zero and short-hours contracts may have originally been a means by which employers and employees could manage unpredictable patterns of work but in recent years have become institutionalized as a form of legal innovation to get around these protections. For workers in this position, no longer does the contract of employment state the actual hours to be worked. All an employer has to do to make a person redundant is to stop phoning them to offer shifts: formal notice periods become irrelevant. The vast majority of employees retain the protections of a contract of employment, but we have a two-tier labour market: one in which the provisions of the Contracts of Employment Act 1963 still hold and one in which they do not.

UNEMPLOYMENT VS EMPLOYMENT

The two charts at the start of this chapter – Figures 1.1 and 1.2 – report slightly different statistics: the first tracks unemployment and the second employment. This distinction reveals an important change in labour market policy in the UK: the shift from focusing on unemployment to employment. Traditionally, economic commentary has focused on the unemployment rate. Reported on the news, and discussed by economists, this was a key measure of the impact of the economy on the lives of ordinary people.

Unemployment as a concept arises from the division of the

population by economists into three groups: employed, unemployed, and inactive, defined as:

- Employed: employees – who work for someone else – and the self-employed;
- Unemployed: out of work and have looked for work in the past four weeks;
- Inactive: everyone else.

The thought process underlying the definition of unemployment is that the only proof of actually wanting work is whether a person has done something to look for it. According to this account, anyone not working but who doesn't want to work isn't a concern for society – they fall into the "inactive" category. Hence, the traditional approach is to be concerned only with the unemployed.

This notion conflicts with reality in two ways.[7] Firstly, people may be discouraged from looking for work because of their frustration in not being able to find a job. In this scenario, the absence of work-seeking activity renders them invisible in the traditional account of unemployment. Secondly, there are lots of people who are in the traditional "inactive" group who might want work (and would actively look for it) if they felt they could overcome barriers to working. Such barriers might be a lack of affordable childcare, lack of care services for older relatives, or disabled people needing adjustments, support, or a lack of discrimination, to help them find and navigate work. The critical point is that the blithe assumption that the absence of work-seeking activity denotes the absence of a concern for society ignores the reality of far too many lives.

This question of whether unemployment or employment matters is not just one of economic statistics but has had an

_____

7 See ILO (2019) for a fuller discussion of problems with the traditional unemployment rate.

important effect on policy and on the labour market as a whole. At the time of the early 1980s recession, the number of people on unemployment benefits rose quickly from 1 million to 3 million and stayed at that level for some years. As a count based on government computer systems, the claimant count is available more quickly than survey-based estimates of unemployment, and so tends to be the figure reported in the media to give an up-to-date indication of trends in the economy. The result was that the figure of 3 million unemployed was a regular staple on evening news bulletins.

One way in which the government of the day responded to this pressure was by moving people from the unemployment rolls to disability benefits. As Figure 1.8 shows, the number of people in receipt of incapacity benefits[8] doubled from around 1.2 million in the mid-1980s to 2.4 million a decade later. Off the unemployment rolls, they were therefore not expected to search for work. In fact, too much work-related activity might be evidence of not being eligible for disability-related benefits, so the incentive was not to look for work. In the absence of any such activity, they were no longer "unemployed" but "inactive" according to the traditional economic definition, and their lack of work was apparently no longer a concern.

There were two important consequences of this flawed analysis. First and foremost, the state assuming people to be permanently out of work meant they were given no support to re-enter work and were expected to remain in that position until reaching retirement age. Even if incapacity benefits are set at a higher rate than unemployment benefits, incomes were still low, compromising living standards and reducing future pension income. Secondly, there were consequences for the wider economy, and for government finances. "Dumping" people onto

8 "Incapacity benefits" are benefits designed to replace some of the income lost through not being able to work because of disability.

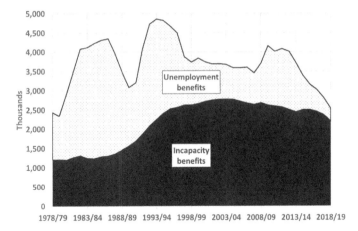

Figure 1.8   Number of people on unemployment and incapacity benefits 1978/79–2018/19

Source: DWP Benefit expenditure tables, 2021.

incapacity benefit represented a contraction in labour supply. Having fewer people available for and seeking work increases business costs and therefore prices faced by consumers, and also reduces business investment. Even though the restriction in labour supply might increase the cash value of wages for some people, overall the poorer performance of the economy and the increase in prices, reduces the spending power of those wages, so real wages are lower. Associated with poorer economic performance are higher costs to government: with more people out of work, total benefit payments are higher and tax receipts are lower.

The Labour government elected in 1997 recognized this problem and declared its intention to change direction. One visible sign of the government's policy intent was through the targets it set itself. The targets for the Department for Work and Pensions (DWP) focused on increasing the employment rate, not reducing the unemployment rate.[9] This change is important because, in its absence, it is much easier to ignore the constraints on women's labour supply from inadequate childcare.

It is notable that economic and labour market policy debate in the United States still largely uses the traditional unemployment rate. For example, the latest Bureau of Labor Statistics news release on the labour market uses this statistic as its most prominent indicator (Bureau of Labor Statistics 2021). There are some who have argued persuasively against this approach (see Blanchflower & Posen 2014) but this focus on the unemployment rate might have something to do with why the US employment rate is so much lower than in the UK.[10]

IDLENESS

According to the *Oxford English Dictionary*, the term idleness can refer to the "state or condition of being…unoccupied" or it can mean "habitual avoidance of work". The tension between the two definitions can be thought of as being rooted in a moral judgement about the nature of being out of work: is it the fault of the individuals in question that they are out of work or does it happen because of the circumstances – the economy, the industry, or the place – in which they find themselves, or their family or health circumstances?

Clearly, one's judgement on these questions will be influenced by prior views about the population and its motivations, and how

---

9   The traditional unemployment rate is *not* the proportion of the population who are unemployed. Traditionally, economists were so convinced that anyone who didn't actively seek work wasn't a problem that they are excluded from the denominator: the formula for the traditional unemployment rate is unemployed/(employed + unemployed).

10 The pre-Covid (2020 Q1) US and UK employment rates for women were 66.6 per cent and 72.5 per cent respectively. For men, the rates in that period were 76.2 per cent and 80.2 per cent (OECD 2021a).

this interacts with political and moral questions. It may help, however, to look at the data on labour market status. Each month, the Labour Force Survey asks people if they have worked in the previous week and, if not, whether they are available to work, have looked for work, and whether they would like work. Figure 1.9 summarizes the results of this survey for October to December 2019 – immediately prior to the Covid-19 recession.

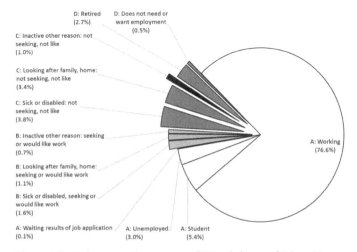

Figure 1.9   Labour market status of UK adults aged 16 to 64, Oct–Dec 2019

Source: Labour Force Survey, Oct–Dec 2019.

The categories in the chart are grouped: those in group A are people who are either participating in the labour market or are preparing themselves to do so. Those in group B are those who are inactive according to economists' classification, but either would like to work or are seeking work. The group C categories are those who are neither seeking work nor would like to work, and the group D segments represent people who have actively chosen not to work because they are retired, or do not need or want work.

From this data we can see that 85 per cent of people are either participating in the labour market or preparing to do so (groups A and B). Apart from those who have actively chosen not to work (group D), only 8 per cent neither want to nor are seeking work, and half of these have a long-term sickness or disability (3.7 per cent), whilst most of the rest are looking after family (3.4 per cent).

So, if idleness means habitual avoidance of work, it applies at best to 1 per cent of the UK's working-age population and does not apply to the vast majority of those without paid work. Did Beveridge use "idleness" in the sense of not having work or in the sense of avoiding it? Either way, given the ambiguity in its definition, and the fact that one of the definitions – "avoiding" work does not apply to most people, it is a phrase that in today's labour market – with its historically high rates of employment – we should move on from.

The result of all the changes in the labour market has been that far too many people are not out of work but stuck in low-paid, low quality, insecure work that offers little prospect of progression such that even two-earner families struggle to afford the necessities of life. Something has clearly gone wrong in our labour market for it to be the case that work is no longer a route to self-sufficiency. If Beveridge were writing today, this would be the challenge he would take on.

2

Productivity

"You make a really good point about the disabled ... There is a group where actually, as you say, they're not worth the full wage ... whether there is something we can do nationally ... if someone wants to work for £2 an hour."

David Freud, Minister for
Welfare Reform, 2014

"We pay the real Living Wage because we see how hard our staff work and there's a value to it ... There are financial benefits in staff retention, better quality of workmanship and actually when you see how hard your staff work, they have to feel valued and I think it's important that your staff feel valued."

Chris Smallwood, owner,
Anchor Removals

In this chapter, we discuss the importance of the UK's productivity problem to low pay and poor job quality. Pay rates arise from an interaction between productivity and worker power and both can contribute to improving wages. However, productivity debates have been bedevilled by a series of assumptions that have led policymakers astray. Firstly, for too long, economists have used a simplified "human capital" model of productivity that assumes that, in the short term, very little can be done about the productivity of an individual worker. What follows from this is the idea expressed by Lord Freud opening this chapter: that the challenge is to set wages at a level low enough that it is still economic to employ that worker. The second error is the obsession with the shiny and new. New inventions can improve national productivity, but often only after their usage is spread across the economy. If this was better understood, perhaps ministers would spend less time posing for photos in front of the National Graphene Institute and more time pounding the high streets of the UK's everyday economy where much of the country's productivity problem actually lies. Finally, for too long, the UK's poor management skills have been an open secret and ignored in economic conversation, having been shut away in the "too difficult" box.

THE UK'S PRODUCTIVITY PROBLEM

Productivity is the amount of output for any given level of input and it can be measured at the level of an individual business or a country as a whole. At the national level, it is normally measured by looking at total economic activity (GDP) per hour worked. The higher productivity the greater the capacity of businesses to reduce costs, capture market share and generate surpluses, which in turn allows payment of higher wages to employees or dividends to shareholders. If productivity is rising then wage rates are able to rise.

Fifty years ago, the UK's productivity was relatively similar to that of France and Germany, but since then it has gradually slipped behind (see Figure 2.1). This relative decline has increased since the global financial crisis in 2008. In the decade before, productivity growth in the UK was amongst the highest amongst the G7 countries of large high-income economies. In the subsequent decade, it was amongst the slowest (ONS 2022).

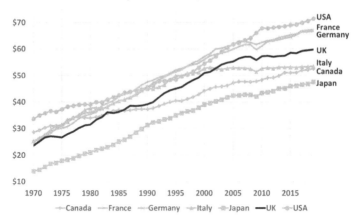

Figure 2.1   Productivity in G7 countries, 1970–2019

Source: OECD.

In the previous chapter, we explored how historically high rates of employment have been accompanied by historically high rates of in-work poverty. Furthermore, although lots of people who are low-paid are not in poverty because they live with higher earners in the household, half of families in in-work poverty have someone who is low paid. So, the problem of low pay is important to in-work poverty. What is more, the UK has more low pay than most similar European countries. As Figure 2.2 shows, amongst higher income countries in Europe, only Germany, the Netherlands and Ireland have higher proportions of employees who are low paid.[1] Naturally, this raises the question of how pay is determined. Why does the UK produce more low-paid workers than most European countries with comparable levels of earnings?

---

1 For this analysis, higher income countries are those with median gross hourly earnings of at least €12 per hour. Low paid means earning below two-thirds of median gross hourly earnings for the country in question.

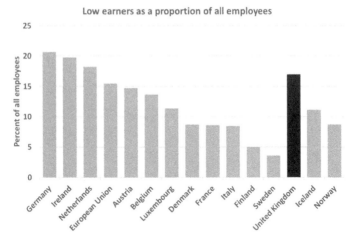

Figure 2.2   Share of low-paid workers in higher income European countries, 2018

Source: Eurostat series EARN_SES_PUB1S, EAR_SES_PUB2S.

It is a standard conclusion of introductory economics that, in a competitive market, workers are paid their marginal product of labour. Essentially, this means that workers get paid the economic value they produce for their employer. The theory behind this notion is that there is a competitive market for workers' labour and, where someone is being paid less than they produce, there is a clear incentive for the employer down the road to make them a higher offer.

Of course, the notion that we do not have a competitive market for labour is the mainstay of research by labour economists. They study how the market deviates from the conditions of perfect competition and the implications of this for employment and wages. The common feature of these departures from the idealized picture is the way in which the balance of power between workers and employers enters the wage equation. In later chapters, we discuss a number of features of the labour market, and services from the state, that have the effect of undermining the power of workers. However, despite the importance of worker power, productivity remains important. As Figure 2.3 shows, productivity growth and wage growth are strongly related, and so productivity is the focus of this chapter.

It stands to reason that any employer who pays their workers as a whole more than they produce for the company cannot afford to stay in business. Thus, productivity sets the ceiling on pay, whereas worker power sets how far below that ceiling pay is actually set. Another way of putting this is that productivity growth tells us how fast wages could rise, but worker power determines how much of the rise will be received by workers as opposed to being retained by employers to be invested or paid to shareholders as profits. That is not to say that specific workers cannot be paid more than their productivity. Employers' misperceptions of individual worker productivity, or preferences for some workers over others, could lead to higher pay for some and lower for others. However, the general proposition that, over the long term, and on average, workers cannot be paid more than the value they produce, still holds.

It is important to be clear what we mean by productivity: it is the amount of value produced for each unit of labour input. The statistical measure that most aligns to this is the economic output per hour of labour. It is notable that cross-country comparisons in public discussion of productivity sometimes look at output per worker. But this is a composite measure that combines productivity – output per hour – and labour supply – hours worked. It is therefore not a pure measure of productivity.

Regrettably, detailed data on output per hour is not as freely available as output per worker. For example, the Office for National Statistics (ONS) Annual Business Survey is only used to produce estimates at firm level of output per worker (ONS 2020), which is far from ideal when trying to understand productivity rather than the combination of productivity and labour supply. So, as

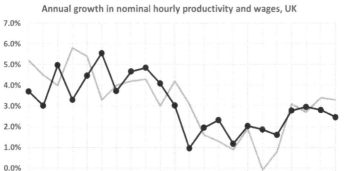

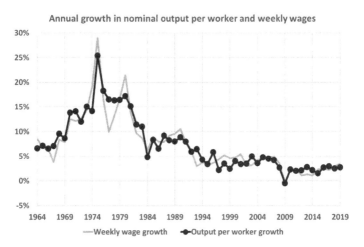

Figure 2.3   Productivity growth and wage growth compared,
1998–2019

Source: (a) ONS time series LZVB inflated by CGBV and Annual Survey of
Hours and Earnings; (b) ONS time series A4YM inflated by CGBV, KAB9
and MD9M.

far as possible, the analysis in this chapter focuses on output per hour, and explores its relationship to hourly pay rates. However, on some occasions, reference is made to output per worker in the absence of more appropriate data.

MINIMUM WAGES

A useful way into considering the relationship between productivity and pay is in relation to minimum wages. Over the past two decades, minimum wages have been introduced or raised significantly in a number of higher income countries (Dube 2019). The welfare benefits of low-paid workers being paid more are pretty obvious. However, traditionally, economists have explained that the biggest risk in minimum-wage policy is of setting the compulsory wage rate at too high a level. This, they contend, will make it uneconomic to employ some workers, resulting in higher unemployment and a contraction in economic activity.

Such thinking has been a constant feature of policy debates since discussion of a national minimum wage in the UK at the end of the 1990s. In 1998, Oliver Letwin, a Conservative MP and later a cabinet minister, raised precisely these arguments in a debate on whether the government should have emergency powers to suspend the minimum wage:

> ... the principal feature of the minimum wage is that it works if it is set at a level where the marginal utility of labour exceeds the minimum wage – where the employer finds that an extra employee earns more for the firm than the minimum wage that must be paid, taking account of the social costs of labour, national insurance contributions and so on. (Hansard HC Deb. 9 March 1998)

The Labour government of the day was particularly concerned not to damage its reputation for economic prudence and therefore sought to provide assurances that the level of the new minimum wage would not be so high as to reduce employment. They set up the Low Pay Commission (LPC) as an independent body with commissioners representing employer and trade union voices with a remit to recommend annually the level of the national minimum wage. The LPC was required to "have regard to: wider economic and social implications; the likely effect on employment and inflation; the impact on competitiveness of business, particularly small firms; and the potential impact on costs to industry and the Exchequer" (Metcalf 1999). The government, and members of the LPC, were at pains to point out the independence and rigour of the process for deciding upon a recommended level for the new minimum wage, reinforcing the point that negative risks to employment and the economy were being managed carefully (Assinder 1998; Metcalf 1999).

By 2015, the concerns of those such as Letwin expressed 15 years earlier had long been forgotten by the Conservative government of the day. In his July Budget in 2015, the Chancellor of the Exchequer, George Osborne, announced with a flourish that he would implement a policy to increase the minimum wage progressively over the following five years to 60 per cent of median earnings:

> Let me be clear: Britain deserves a pay rise and Britain is getting a pay rise. I am today introducing a new national living wage. We will set it to reach £9 an hour by 2020. The new national living wage will be compulsory. Working people aged 25 and over will receive it. It will start next April at the rate of £7.20. The Low Pay Commission will recommend future rises that achieve the Government's objective of reaching 60 per cent of median earnings by 2020. (Hansard HC Deb. 8 July 2015)

Crucially, he was announcing his intention to ignore both the content and the process of advice from the LPC. The LPC had recommended that the main rate of the minimum wage should be £6.70 per hour for the year from October 2015 (Low Pay Commission 2015) whereas Osborne introduced a rate of £7.20 from April 2016. He also pre-announced that over the following few years, the level would be increased progressively to 60 per cent of median hourly earnings by 2020 – at that time estimated to be £9 per hour (HM Treasury 2015a).[2] In fact, sluggish earnings growth over the following few years meant that the minimum wage only exceeded £9 per hour from April 2022.

The important point in relation to process is that, instead of waiting for a report each year from the LPC before making any statements about the likely level of the minimum wage, Osborne was pre-announcing the intention to reach 60 per cent of median earnings by 2020. No longer, therefore, was this the careful dance of being seen to listen to the latest economic analysis before setting a rate designed not to scare the economic horses. Although the government may have felt confident to abandon the economic caution of the previous two decades, the UK's official economic forecaster – the Office for Budget Responsibility (OBR) – took the view that the new policy would cost 60,000 jobs by 2020, and reduce GDP by 0.2 per cent (OBR 2015).

The underlying conceptual basis of the notion that there is negative effect of minimum wages on employment is that, in the short term, each worker has an inherent level of productivity. Over the medium to long term, this inherent productivity, or "human capital", can be improved through training or by experience. However, without these inputs, each worker's productivity is essentially fixed. This conceptualization leads inevitably to the conclusion that, if the worker's pay rate is set above their level of productivity, it is uneconomic to employ them.

---

2 George Osborne renamed the new 25-and-over rate (23-and-over from April 2021) of the National Minimum Wage as the "National Living Wage" and it is referred to by this name in official documents.

It was precisely this thought process that lay behind the comments, quoted earlier, of the government minister David Freud, that it would be uneconomic to employ some disabled people as the value that they could produce would be less than prevailing wage rates (Watt & Wintour 2014). The implication for the minimum wage is clear: set it above the (inherent) productivity level of some workers and they will be rendered effectively unemployable as no firm can afford to employ them without losing money.

However, the evidence of the past two decades suggests strongly that the traditional economic argument does not hold. In 2019, Arin Dube was commissioned by Philip Hammond, the Chancellor of the Exchequer, to review international evidence on minimum wages (Hansard HC Deb. 13 March 2019). His findings were that minimum wages had not generally reduced employment (Dube 2019). The implication is that employers had been able to find ways of improving productivity so as to be able to afford to pay higher ways without having to cut jobs. So, the notion that little can boost productivity apart from long years of experience or expensive training courses is certainly incorrect.

FRONTIER FIRMS VS EVERYDAY ECONOMY

To understand this argument in more depth, it is helpful to look at the context in which policy discussions on productivity take place. From 1970 to 2007 (just before the Global Financial Crisis), productivity growth in the UK averaged 2.2 per cent per year. Between 2009 (after the GFC) and 2019 (before the Covid-19 recession), this had fallen to 1.3 per cent a year (OECD 2021b).

The question of how to improve productivity growth is normally thought of as a macroeconomic issue where, if skills are not the answer, then innovation – the development of new methods, ideas and technologies – is thought to be the most significant driver. Indeed, it is rare that a government announcement on productivity isn't accompanied by a visit to, or at least a mention of, the National Graphene Institute in Manchester,[3] home of research into the new "wonder material".[4]

Despite the ministerial erosion of pavements in Manchester, there is strong evidence that innovation, or lack of it, is not the cause of the UK's productivity problems. Analysis by Andy Haldane and others at the Bank of England has shown that this slowdown in productivity growth was not restricted to particular sectors of the economy but was fairly widespread. Furthermore, shifts in economic activity from higher productivity manufacturing to lower productivity services cannot explain the productivity growth slowdown. The answers lie in looking at the distribution of productivity amongst firms (Haldane 2017).

What the Bank of England analysis shows is that there is a large and growing disparity in productivity performance between so-called "frontier" firms – the top 5–10 per cent of firms – which continued to see steady productivity growth between 2002 and 2014 and the bottom 60 per cent which saw virtually no growth over this period, and there was very modest growth amongst firms in the fourth quintile.

Importantly, the UK does not lack for frontier firms – highly innovative and productive companies. Further analysis by the Bank of England found the productivity levels of the top 10 per cent of UK companies are at least 100 per cent above the median whereas in France and Germany it is 80 per cent and 60 per cent respectively (Haldane 2018). The Bank of England view is that "it is non-frontier companies that largely explain flatlining productivity over recent years" (Haldane 2017).

A key question that follows from this is where should the efforts of the state go to improve productivity. One account is that, if the UK already has as many or more highly productive

---

3 For example, see visits from George Osborne (BBC News 2015) and President Xi Jinping (Fitzgerald 2015).

4 See https://www.graphene-info.com/graphene-introduction.

frontier firms as comparable countries, innovation at the frontiers of knowledge is not the UK's problem. Given that enough companies in the UK are already making a good fist of competing with the best of the rest of the world, does the state have much more to offer in this area?

The implication from this view is that efforts to boost the UK's economic performance should not focus on high-tech firms but on what some people have called the "everyday" economy – the long-tail of less productive firms. Rather than roaming the streets of Manchester in search of graphene, ministers should be walking down local high streets and industrial estates in search of how to help the ordinary firms that explain more of the UK's productivity gap with comparable countries.

However, there are two counterarguments to this view. Firstly, what if the presence of frontier firms has the effect of driving up average wage levels in an area such that the low-paying businesses – whether coffee shops or cleaning firms – are forced to pay higher wages in order to attract any staff at all. In this circumstance, perhaps the requirement to pay higher wages might force them to look for productivity improvements to justify those wages.

This question was looked at explicitly in a study by Neil Lee and Stephen Clarke. They examined whether and how residents benefit from growth of high-technology industries in their local economy. They found that high-tech growth does increase the number of jobs available to local people with lower levels of skills, with every ten high-tech jobs creating around seven local jobs in the service sector. Of these, around six go to local residents with lower levels of skills. However, these new jobs are typically low paid and, if anything, lower the average wage available to low-skilled workers. The effects for mid-skilled workers is slightly different: they do not benefit from higher employment but do see a gain in wages (Lee & Clarke 2019).

The implication of this study is that boosting high-tech jobs might create more barista and cleaning jobs, but it doesn't necessarily provide routes out of low pay and in-work poverty for people with lower levels of skills. What follows is that a government seeking to use productivity to boost wages for low-paid workers must focus on what Haldane has called the "long tail" of less productive firms.

A further argument against focusing on the long tail of less productive firms is that they occupy too small a proportion of the economy to be worth bothering with. Oliveira-Cunha *et al*. (2021) (Resolution Foundation and Centre for Economic Performance) argue that, for the bottom 40 per cent of firms as measured by productivity per worker, weighted by numbers of staff, a 10 per cent increase in their productivity would only add 1.2 per cent to GDP. On the other hand, the same boost at the top of the productivity distribution would boost GDP by 7.5 per cent.

It is unquestionably the case that an equivalent percentage rise in productivity at the top of the distribution compared to the bottom will do more for aggregate productivity. However, is it realistic to expect similar levels of productivity growth at the top and bottom? We have already seen that the UK's frontier firms already compete with the best in the world: arguably there is not much "low-hanging fruit" – obvious changes that might improve productivity – for these firms to identify and implement.

In 2015, the CIPD launched a pilot project to offer two days of free human resources (HR) consultancy to small businesses in three locations: Hackney, Stoke-on-Trent and Glasgow (CIPD 2017). The expectation was that the project would help to improve strategic HR decision-making within small businesses such as making investments in project management and leadership capability, or in helping to deliver transformational change. However, the experience of the pilot was that the support sought by small businesses was far more about getting the basics of HR processes right. Owner-managers were concerned about their ability to ensure that their HR processes were legal and correct, and used the support offered in this pilot to address these issues, rather than bring about strategic or transformational change. They also felt that this support improved productivity within their businesses.

One of the key messages from this study is that the "long tail" of less productive businesses do have substantial amounts of "low-hanging fruit" when it comes to improving productivity. In this case, even something as simple as free HR advice to improve basic processes led to a perception of increases in productivity. As the CIPD evaluation report notes, there is substantial potential for wider rollout of support of this kind for small businesses and therefore potential for widespread improvements in productivity at a relatively modest cost (CIPD 2017).

One further point about the Resolution Foundation/Centre for Economic Performance argument is that the Bank of England analysis that they were arguing against actually said that the bottom 60 per cent of firms had had virtually no productivity growth over the 12 years to 2014, and that growth in the next 20 per cent had also been very modest. In other words, the "long tail" is not just the bottom 40 per cent of firms but a significant majority. This renders the point that the bottom 40 per cent might only contribute a small amount to aggregate growth less helpful in determining where the focus of policy should rest.

Ultimately, the question of where to focus policy – whether at the top or the bottom of the productivity distribution – depends on two key variables. Firstly, which part of the distribution has the most potential to increase its productivity beyond the current level of performance and, secondly, where can government be most effective in supporting businesses to make changes over and above what they would have done anyway. What is clear is that the idea of donning a white coat and inventing the future is persuasive – ministers can't resist it – even if the evidence behind focusing on frontier firms is partial at best.

MANAGEMENT

So, we know that the UK has large differences in productivity between its frontier, or most productive, firms and the rest. What else do we know about why the UK's productivity gap with other countries exists? A traditional way to look at productivity gaps is to break them down into three potential causes: capital intensity, labour quality, and everything else (known by economists as total factor productivity). Capital intensity means the amounts spent per worker on kit of all kind: equipment, IT, etc, and labour quality is usually defined as formal qualifications. Total factor productivity is the bit left over after capital intensity and formal qualifications and can include how well the tools, equipment and IT are used, how well people are managed, and how work is organized.

In 2018, John Forth and Ana Rincon Aznar sought to use this classification to break down the UK's productivity gap in low-waged sectors compared with France, Germany and the United States. What they found was that, across low-waged sectors, the largest explanation of the gap was in total factor productivity, rather than capital intensity or (to some degree) labour quality. This is an important finding because, in other sectors of the economy, capital intensity is more important as an explanation of the UK's differences with other countries.

For several years, Nicholas Bloom and Jon van Reenen used surveys to collect management practice data from firms across several countries with a view to analysing the drivers of productivity (Bloom & Van Reenen 2007). They concluded that management practices are "significantly associated" with higher productivity and, furthermore, that 30 per cent of cross-country differences in total factor productivity, and differences between firms within countries, can be explained by differences in management practices (Bloom *et al*. 2017).

Further insight into the potential for improved management

practices to deliver productivity gains comes from the voluntary
Living Wage (called the Real Living Wage).[5] Each year, based on
analysis by the Resolution Foundation (Cominetti 2020), the
Living Wage Foundation publishes a new rate for the Real Living
Wage, and campaigns for companies to adopt this standard as
their minimum. As Figure 2.4 shows, this movement has now gone
sufficiently far that there is a visible spike in the distribution of
hourly earnings at the level of the Real Living Wage.

Figure 2.4   Distribution of UK hourly earnings, 2021

Source: ONS, Annual Survey of Hours and Earnings.

At the end of October 2021, of private sector companies that
had adopted the Real Living Wage, 236 were in the care industry, 138 in cleaning, 354 in hospitality, and 279 in retail (Living
Wage Foundation 2021). Whereas a banking or consultancy firm
that employs very few low-paid workers might find it relatively

---

5 Called the "Real Living Wage" to distinguish from the statutory minimum wage, which is officially called the "National Living Wage" – an
   audacious land-grab of the phrase "living wage" by George Osborne in
   his July 2015 Budget.

inexpensive to increase wages for a small proportion of their staff, industries such as care, cleaning, hospitality and retail are all highly competitive and, on average, low paid.

An evaluation by Cardiff Business School of motivations for, and implications of, implementing the Real Living Wage found that most companies do so for values-led or reputational reasons and do not make any associated changes to management practices: they were happy to absorb the additional costs. However, employers in low-pay sectors were most likely to make changes to practices, including additional training or promotion opportunities (Heery *et al*. 2017). Thus, in those sectors where competitive pressures make paying higher wages hardest to achieve, those employers who have done so have been able to justify the change through improved management.

Of course, the Real Living Wage example applies only to companies that have chosen voluntarily to sign up for change, often for values-led or reputational reasons. To what extent does the potential for improvements in management practices exist across the rest of the economy?

In 2018, Anne Green and others found that, in low-wage sectors, firms had only "a partial understanding of productivity" and were, in general, unable to describe its relationship to wages. Staff availability and retention, local pay norms, and the legal minimum, were more likely to drive wage setting. Effectively, increases in the legal minimum wage precipitated employers to look for productivity improvements. However, few looked at skills development or long-term investments to achieve this: those who perceived themselves to have a low-wage low-skills business model felt no incentive to do so (Green *et al*. 2018). This finding reinforces the experience of the CIPD People Skills pilot project discussed earlier: that many owner-managers are less focused on long-term strategic development of their businesses but on managing day-to-day pressures. They set wages according to external drivers – market and legal – and respond by looking for productivity improvements as and when necessary to afford wage increases.

BREXIT

An important part of the UK's recent economic story is Brexit – the biggest economic change in several decades – and it is worth considering whether it will have any impact on low pay and productivity. There are two potential mechanisms by which this might happen: immigration and trade.

On immigration, there is one argument that says that, with reduced immigration from the European Union, there might be less competition amongst workers for the available jobs so that remaining workers can secure higher wages. The issue, however, is that immigration doesn't just reduce the supply of labour but also the demand. If there are fewer people in the UK looking to buy goods and services, there are likely to be fewer jobs available, and this would tend to reduce wages.

The most significant analysis on how these effects might balance out was carried out by Stephen Nickell and Jumana Salaheen for the Bank of England (2015). Their study found that effects on employment rates are negligible and that it would take extremely large increases in immigration to produce a small downward effect on wages. So, the expectation is that, unless Brexit prompts very large amounts of outmigration, there is unlikely to be noticeable positive effects on wages.

When it comes to trade, the OBR reported in March 2022 that Brexit appears so far to be on course to reducing the UK's trade intensity – the share of its economy accounted for by trade – by 15 per cent (OBR 2022: 62). Generally speaking, increasing trade intensity increases productivity. So, the expectation is that productivity growth will be slowed by the UK's reduced trade intensity.

The long and short of these Brexit effects is that they are not likely in themselves to produce an increase in wage rates, and are likely to reduce productivity growth. It therefore becomes even more important for the government to get to grips with the factors driving the UK's productivity problem.

CONCLUSION

So where does this discussion leave us? Firstly, although productivity is not the only explanation for low pay, it is an important part of the picture. Whereas most industries in the UK experience a gap in productivity compared to similar countries, in low-paid industries the explanation for this is more likely to be the quality of management. This insight, combined with the experience of high levels of employment despite an increasing minimum wage, suggests that the traditional account of productivity is inadequate for the UK. Workers do not have an inherent level of productivity based on their "human capital" that policy needs to anticipate: management is likely to be a much more important driver of how much an individual worker can produce for a firm. Wages are not simply the result of productivity levels but may actually be the cause of higher productivity because they can induce more effort to improve management practices.

Furthermore, the lack of "trickle-down" from frontier firms to improvements in low-paid work suggests that policy on productivity needs to focus on diffusion of management skills to non-frontier firms. This is a very different policy agenda to the traditional triumvirate of innovation, infrastructure and skills. However, the challenges of stimulating wider adoption of improved management practices are considerable. Many small companies have little idea of their own productivity – wages are set through informal rules of thumb and adherence to externally-set rules such as the legal minimum wage, or with reference to local norms. Their needs for support on management issues are at a very basic level: the challenges of running a business in a tough economic climate and staying on the right side of employment law are sufficient to occupy many small business owners, giving them little capacity for making the case to themselves for investment in management skills or practices. Initiatives such as Be the Business and the CIPD People Skills pilot offer a likely direction for solutions. However, much more needs to be understood about the reality of running ordinary, everyday businesses to make any support from the state effective.

Finally, there is a complementarity between solving low pay and addressing the UK's principle macroeconomic weakness: productivity. However, to do so effectively means getting out of the macroeconomic tramlines within which productivity debates normally exist. Ministers need to stop telling themselves that visiting high tech research institutes will solve the UK's productivity problem and start visiting the businesses that haven't had any productivity growth for a decade. That's where the problem exists and that's where it needs solving.

3

Good work

If we accept that productivity plays an important role in creating the potential for higher wage growth for low-paid workers, and that better management is key to improving this, the next question has to be how might we achieve this?

It turns out that there is already an answer to this question ready and waiting in the form of "Good Work". Gaining momentum in recent years as a response to growing insecurity in the labour market, the Good Work movement offers both a view on the practices that are necessary to improve workplaces, and examples of practical action having been taken to increase standards across the economy. In this chapter, we chart the progress of the Good Work movement and consider what else needs to be done to get the UK out of its low-pay, low-productivity rut.

Policy interest in "good" or "decent" work is not new and indeed pre-dates the Beveridge Report. Established in 1919, the International Labour Organization (ILO) brought together governments, employers and workers in order to set labour standards, develop policies and devise programmes that promote decent work for all. In 1944, the ILO's Declaration of Philadelphia set out the key principles for the ILO's work after the end of the Second World War. The Declaration states clearly that "poverty anywhere constitutes a danger to prosperity everywhere", and includes commitments to promote programmes that will achieve living wages and "ensure a just share of the fruits of progress to all". It also highlighted the importance of job satisfaction, well-being, and "the cooperation of management and labour in the continuous improvement of productive efficiency" (ILO 1944).

But although the notion of good or decent work has been with us for a while, its profile in policy debates has grown more recently in the UK context and internationally as job opportunities have polarized, working conditions have worsened and work has become increasingly precarious (Osterman 2013). In addition to low pay, poor quality insecure work (including zero-hours contracts and bogus self-employment[1]), a lack of progression opportunities for low-paid workers and low productivity are all now high-profile issues on the UK policy agenda.

Alongside political pressure resulting from the high profile rise of zero-hours contracts and poor working conditions in the gig economy, policymakers have increasingly become interested in promoting "good work" as part of efforts to improve productivity outcomes. In 2017, UK Prime Minister Theresa May commissioned Matthew Taylor to review working practices and to make recommendations on how to promote good work. Good work received several mentions in the UK government's white paper Industrial Strategy published later that year (BEIS 2017) and in 2018, the government published its own Good Work Plan (BEIS 2018).

But what does "good work" actually mean? It sounds like a great idea – after all, nobody wants bad work. However, the concept tends to be defined into one of two ways. One approach is to look at the characteristics of a job against an objective standard

---

1 Commentators use the term "bogus self employment" where employers compel staff to be self-employed in order to avoid paying the minimum wage, national insurance, sick pay, holiday pay and pension contributions (see Citizens Advice 2015).

– for example, whether a job provides access to flexible working. Another approach is to look at employees' perceptions of their job, such as whether they feel supported by their managers. In both approaches, opinions will vary about how to design the standard. For example, in the former case, debate might centre on whether to include the Real Living Wage in the criteria. In the latter case, decisions need to be taken about which subjective perceptions to include and their relative importance in any composite index.

Note that good work does not refer to the nature of the tasks required. For example, one job might be considered by some to be more desirable because it involves working in a warm, comfortable office rather than outdoors in the cold at night. Rather, good work refers to the employment conditions and management practices that surround those tasks: whether flexible working might be available, or whether managers are effective in supporting workers.

Regardless of these debates, of necessity, operationalizing "good work" involves defining a set of standards for employment practices, and then encouraging or incentivizing adoption. Importantly, in many places where Good Work standards have been created – such as in Greater Manchester (see below), standards have been devised as a collaboration between the state, employers and unions and workers themselves. Good Work is a shared agenda that they are all a part of.

While different concepts and frameworks have led to slightly different approaches, ultimately, the most practical applications have similar dimensions. In 2018 the Measuring Job Quality Working Group was brought together by the Carnegie Trust and Royal Society of Arts to develop an agreed set of job quality measures in response to the Taylor Review's recommendation that the UK needed a standard measure. Building on the work of the CIPD the group identified seven broad dimensions of good work (see Table 3.1).

Terms of employment	Job security, minimum guaranteed hours, underemployment
Pay and benefits	Pay (actual), satisfaction with pay, entitlements, non-wage benefits
Health, safety and psychosocial well-being	Health and safety, physical injury, mental health
Job design and nature of work	Training, usefulness of training, use of skills, control, opportunities for progression, sense of purpose, autonomy and discretion
Social support and cohesion	Peer support, line manager relationship, personal development, resolving problems
Voice and representation	Trade union membership, employee information, employee involvement
Work–life balance	Over-employment, Overtime (paid and unpaid), Flexibility (formal and informal), suitability of hours, advance notice of shift patterns and work location, anxiety and work–life balance

Table 3.1   Seven dimensions of job quality

Source: Carnegie Trust/RSA; Irvine *et al.* (2018).

Once we have a view on what good work is, how do we make it happen? It is notable that, despite recent policy interest, the decent work movement is largely one that is taking place away from Westminster and Whitehall. Campaigns led by the third sector, local governments and broader civil society have increasingly centred on the Good Work agenda. Among the highest profile is the living wage campaign and more recent developments in the establishment of Good Employment Charters by local policymakers in several areas in the UK. We take a look at each of these in turn before considering what more needs to be done on the part of the state to support this agenda.

PAYING A LIVING WAGE

The Living Wage Foundation has been campaigning for wages based on their calculation of the real cost of living – encouraging employers to adopt voluntarily a higher pay floor to reflect that "a hard day's work deserves a fair day's pay". Based on a public consultation method called the Minimum Income Standard, the Real Living Wage currently stands at £9.50 across the UK and £10.85 in London (compared to the statutory minimum wage of £8.91 for over 23s and £8.36 for under 23s).[2] Since its inception in 2001 more than 7,000 employers have become Living Wage Employers and over 250,000 employees have received a pay rise as a result.[3]

Paying the Real Living Wage is voluntary. As discussed in the previous chapter, many employers are motivated to become Real Living Wage employers as it aligns with their values or mission to be socially responsible or for reputational reasons. But there is also a compelling business case for becoming a Real Living Wage employer. In a survey of over 840 businesses in 2016, Edmund Heery and colleagues (2017) found that 93 per cent of employers feel they have benefitted from accreditation. Paying a Real Living Wage brings reputational benefits – which is not only helpful both for attracting and retaining staff but also in terms of broader corporate branding. Employers interviewed in research by Calum Carson recognize the improvements it can make to employee recruitment and retention, alongside its role in improving relationships with staff: "The longer we can keep people, the more productive we can make them, the less we have to pay on training,

---

2 Note that the statutory minimum wage for over-23s is, confusingly, referred to by the government as the "National Living Wage" but is entirely separate from the "Real Living Wage", calculated and recommended by the Living Wage Foundation.

3 See https://www.livingwage.org.uk/.

the less we have to pay on recruitment. So, to us it's just common sense to pay it" (construction employer cited in Carson 2021).

Although a small number of employers, who have adopted the Real Living Wage, report some challenges due to an increase in the wage bill (most typically those in lower paying sectors), most do not report any significant negative effects and have been able to absorb higher wage costs without making major changes to the way their businesses are run. And there is limited evidence that employers reduce other positive aspects of employment contracts in order to compensate them for higher wage bills.

This voluntary effort to increase the quality of work is clearly beneficial to the lowest paid workers who see a pay rise as the result of it. Some local governments and other tendering organizations have also incentivized living wage adoption by adding specific clauses that contractors must pay the Real Living Wage, so being able to secure contracts is also a key benefit. However, this voluntary approach can only take us so far. Furthermore, although raising the bar below which wages should not fall, it also does nothing to support continued progression for those earning above this level.

Aside from pay, there are broader efforts to promote good employment more holistically. Here, devolved and subnational policymakers have gone much further than central government in promoting the Good Work agenda, for example through the Good Employment Charter in Greater Manchester (see Box 3.1) and the establishment of the Fair Work Convention – an advisory body set up to inform Scottish ministers. A Fair Work Commission has also been set up by the Welsh First Minister, and good work charters and standards are in development across the country, for example in the Liverpool City Region and West Yorkshire Combined Authority.

These initiatives are relatively new and monitoring and evaluating their impact will be critical for understanding their effectiveness. Meeting the particular standards will clearly be more challenging in some sectors than others. However, what they have done is demonstrate a clear appetite amongst policy-makers, workers, unions and employers to embrace the Good Work agenda, and the challenges need to be recognized, understood and overcome.

BOX 3.1 GOOD WORK CASE STUDY: GREATER MANCHESTER GOOD EMPLOYMENT CHARTER

The Greater Manchester Good Employment Charter is a voluntary membership and assessment scheme created by the Greater Manchester Combined Authority that aims to raise employment standards across Greater Manchester, for all organizations of any size, sector or geography. Shaped by consultation with employers, employees and other key stakeholder groups in Greater Manchester, the Charter identifies seven key characteristics of good employment: secure work, flexible work, Real Living Wage, engagement and voice, recruitment, people management, health and well-being. The principles of equality, diversity, and inclusion cut across all characteristics. The Charter has two "tiers": The supporter tier, which includes employers that "support the aim of the Charter and have made a commitment to improving practice in all characteristics of good employment" and the members tier, which includes employers that "have made the Supporter Commitment and meet the membership criteria in all characteristics of the Charter".

WHAT ABOUT MANAGEMENT?

Earlier we talked about the importance of management. But where does management come into the good work debate? Well, many of the dimensions of good work standards clearly require better quality management. The leadership of firms has also been identified as central to their productivity. However, as noted earlier, the UK performs poorly in this regard. UK businesses don't spend enough time and resources investing in leadership and broader human capital development (Danker 2020).

There is therefore a need for interventions focused specifically on improving management practices, however providing the right interventions for small and medium-sized enterprises (SMEs) in particular has proven challenging. Fortunately, activity is underway to try and meet this challenge. Be the Business, for example, is a government-supported and industry-led initiative, which provides targeted support and guidance for UK business leaders looking to improve their practices. Taking a test-and-learn approach, they are attempting to identify which interventions are effective in driving SME productivity. Work is ongoing, but they claim a range of positive impacts which, while driven by productivity-enhancing objectives, may also have led to improvements in the working lives of their staff.

For example, by introducing what are rather standard aspects of management and leadership practice (e.g. setting targets and introducing regular performance reviews), SME leaders have opened up more space for dialogue with their employees. This has made employees feel more involved and valued, as well as impacting positively on their bottom line (Danker 2020). Partnerships between academics, policymakers and business communities have also resulted in a range of interventions designed to try and improve management practices. Box 3.2 summarizes some of this recent activity in more detail.

THE RELATIONSHIP BETWEEN GOOD
WORK AND PRODUCTIVITY

In 2020, Derek Bosworth and Chris Warhurst reviewed the evidence on good work and its effect on productivity. They point out the challenges of examining the relationship between the two

BOX 3.2 CASE STUDY:
IMPROVING MANAGEMENT PRACTICES
Good Employment Learning Lab

The Good Employment Learning Lab (GELL), led by Professor Julia Rouse at Manchester Metropolitan University, is a project funded by the Economic and Social Research Council (ESRC) to develop and test the most effective ways of supporting line managers to manage people. Manchester Met HR experts are delivering a fully funded training programme for line managers across Greater Manchester and the North West to understand and tackle a variety of management challenges. Learning Labs provide spaces where researchers, policymakers, practitioners and managers can collaborate to understand and address shared problems. They frame ideas for better practice founded on robust theories of change, experiment with interventions that can logically achieve change and evaluate "what works". At a deeper level, Learning Labs support long-term, trusting and creative relationships and use learning from particular experiments to think about how to address "tricky" problems.

Productivity from Below

The Productivity from Below project, also funded by the ESRC, is led by Professor Monder Ram at Aston University. The project focuses on strengthening management practices in micro-businesses. Building on research coproduced with practitioners it is designing and implementing evidence-based interventions to boost productivity. Customized programmes will be designed to upgrade leadership and management skills. Alongside this, the project aims to support the development of a more responsive and inclusive business support ecosystem in the West-Midlands.

People Skills

People Skills was a UK pilot programme (2015–16) delivered through the CIPD and local partners. The programme provided small firms in Hackney (London), Stoke-on-Trent and Glasgow with free HR support and advice, provided by a small bank of independent HR consultants. Businesses participating in the programme could also make use of the CIPD's HR Inform online support system. An evaluation of the programme demonstrates high demand for HR support amongst SMEs, alongside the effectiveness of a model based on bespoke, face-to-face provision to meet this. The project found that small firms' people management needs were largely quite basic (for example, contracts, legal compliance), and thus the People Skills pilots were helpful in allowing employers to "get the people management basics right", which was felt to provide the foundation for more transformational change (See CIPD 2017).

given the absence of datasets that allow the analysis of the two sets of variables together, alongside the inconsistencies in defining job quality and the range of productivity measures. However, they conclude that on the whole the two are positively correlated. More specifically, they found a positive correlation with productivity in four of the five dimensions of good work for which evidence exists (pay and benefits; health, safety and psycho-social well-being; job design and the nature of work; and work–life balance).

On the dimension of voice and representation, they conclude that the "existing evidence appears mixed but not discouraging".

Looking at some of the sub-indicators of good work, they also found that the opportunity to use knowledge (part of job design and nature of work) and teamwork (part of social support and cohesion) are both strongly positively related to productivity. We return to skills utilization in Chapter 8.

Significantly, when looking at the issue conversely, they find stronger correlations between bad work and poor productivity. More broadly, researchers have increasingly drawn links between low productivity, low pay, and insecure work (Innes 2018). The employment consultancy Timewise highlight evidence that shows the positive value of "genuine, two-way flexible working" in terms of attracting talent and improving retention, alongside boosting inclusion and diversity, and supporting women and other under-represented groups to progress to senior levels (Stewart 2020). They highlight reports from individual businesses that increases in productivity were observed where staff work flexibly: for example, a survey by British Telecom in 2014 found that the productivity of flexible workers increased by 30 per cent (Unison 2014).

WHERE NEXT?

It is clear that there are mechanisms for tackling in-work poverty while at the same time improving productivity: the answer is more widespread adoption of Good Work standards. The Good Work movement demonstrates that there is an appetite among employers and policymakers to improve employment practices proactively. But while the Good Work movement in its various guises has made a start, and certainly plays an important role in engaging businesses, ultimately there are limits to what these voluntary measures can achieve. Both the Real Living Wage and employment charters are ultimately voluntary initiatives that cannot be enforced. The Real Living Wage campaign's role in tackling in-work poverty, although important, is only partial. It is notable that many large employers, who could clearly do so, have not yet signed up. In the UK higher education sector, for example, only 35 universities were accredited in 2021 (Carson 2021). Similarly, as Ceri Hughes and colleagues (2017) note, "Charters should not be relied on to tackle long-term structural issues within the labour market".

The question is what should government do to make this happen? Should it be encouraging or promoting it? Or, should it go further and enforce or require it?

The Taylor Review championed "the British way", appearing broadly satisfied with how the UK labour market currently operates. But as we show later in this book, the UK lags behind in its enforcement of labour market rules and its resistance to labour market regulation is misguided. The Taylor Review was also roundly criticized for its failure to grasp the lack of power and choice available to many workers in today's labour market (Moore *et al.* 2018).

Despite its shortcomings, the Taylor Review did signal recognition among policymakers about the importance of good work. However, while the Good Work movement outside of Westminster has continued to build momentum, national progress has stalled. In 2021, the position of Director of Labour Market Enforcement – an important government position created to lead a crackdown on labour market abuse – was left vacant for ten months, despite Matthew Taylor's offer to remain in place, unpaid, as interim when his term came to an end in January 2021. Concerns are mounting about what will happen to employment rights in the light of the UK's departure from the European Union, and as the greatly anticipated Employment Bill has been repeatedly kicked down the road (Strauss 2021). At a minimum central government should adopt procurement rules that give credit for adoption of appropriate standards. The question of how much further to go will be examined in the chapter on regulation and enforcement.

4

Supporting people into work: a brief history

So far we have discussed the importance of productivity to pay rates and the quality of work, demonstrating the need to improve productivity in the everyday economy through better management, and focusing on good work as a means of doing so. Now, we shall look at the other side of the employment relationship: namely, the power that people have over the nature and quality of the work they do. Examining the state's actions across a range of policy areas, we ask whether they empower or disempower the unemployed and low paid.

We start by examining policies to support people into work, and how these have developed over time. Normally, these policies are examined in very simple terms through their effectiveness or otherwise in enabling entries into work. Today, however, with job quality, low pay and limited pay progression being a much more important part of the UK labour market story, it becomes important to examine how policies to support people into work affect the quality of work people move into, and what happens to people after they have entered the workplace. We start by looking at the history of such policies, then examine the realities of today's offer, and finally look at better ways to approach this crucial area of policy.

BEVERIDGE AND THE 1940S

Since the beginning of the modern National Insurance system on 5 July 1948, the state has provided both unemployment insurance and welfare payments to workless families without other sources of income.[1] Although the purpose of these financial transfers has been to prevent extreme poverty, there was also recognition of the need for recipients to minimize their draw upon the state by looking for work.

Both Beveridge and the wartime government agreed that people who were unemployed should receive support from a placement service to help them find work (Clarke 1944), and that unemployment insurance should not be paid unconditionally and indefinitely. However, there were differences in views about what should happen after the expiry of the initial period. Beveridge said that "Unemployment benefit will continue at the same rate without means test so long as unemployment lasts, but will normally be subject to a condition of attendance at a work or training centre after a certain period" (Beveridge 1942). In contrast, the government wanted to limit unemployment insurance to 30 weeks, with families needing to rely on National Assistance (the means-tested benefit of the day) after that period (Clarke 1944).

The themes from the debates of 1942 resonate today. The state has a clear interest in people who are unemployed returning to work: people are better off, the economy is stronger, tax revenues are higher and benefit expenditure is lower. Given this interest, it was expected at that time, and is expected now, that the state would take a role in providing support to people to find work. Second, the question of conditionality was a live one in political

---

1 Unemployment insurance for a single person was set at 26 shillings per week whilst National Assistance – the means-tested support for those not eligible for insurance – was 24 shillings per week (Hemming *et al.* 1965).

and policy debate then as now: what should people be required to do to receive benefits?

In the opening chapter, we discussed the different moral judgements that one can make about the nature of unemployment. The same question applies here: is it the fault of the individuals in question that they are out of work, or does it happen because of the circumstances – the economy, the industry or the place – in which they find themselves? For policymakers more inclined to the "circumstances" narrative, it makes more sense to concentrate on improving the support provided to people who are unemployed. For those inclined to the "fault" narrative, it is unsurprising that there is more focus on conditionality.

INCREASING CONDITIONALITY: THE 1980S

Between the 1960s and early 1980s, work-search requirements for claiming unemployment benefit actually fell. Van Reenen (2003) reports that the number of referrals of unemployed people for not seeking work fell by 80 per cent between 1968 and 1976. In 1982, cutbacks in public expenditure meant that the requirement to visit a job centre was withdrawn. Furthermore, as discussed in Chapter 1, people were increasingly encouraged to move off the unemployment rolls and onto disability benefits on a large scale. However, by the mid-to-late 1980s conditionality began to feature in the welfare system in a more significant way. Influenced by new right thinkers such as Charles Murray (1984) and Lawrence Mead (1992), concern about cultures of dependency began to feature more prominently in policy debate and development (see Dwyer *et al.* forthcoming for a helpful overview).

In 1986, compulsory six-monthly interviews were introduced for people who had been unemployed for at least six months and the disqualification period for people deemed to have left work voluntarily was increased from six to 13 weeks, and later to six months.

The Social Security Act 1989 outlined the requirement that those in receipt of unemployment benefits should accept any job and were not permitted to turn down jobs on the grounds of inadequate pay, or because it did not align with their skills or experience. Claimants were expected to "actively seek work", not just "be available for work". The introduction of Jobseekers' Agreements following the Jobseekers Act of 1995 made this more explicit (Dwyer *et al*. forthcoming).

SUPPORT WITH CONDITIONALITY: THE 2000S

In 1997, the Labour Party came into government promising an ambitious "welfare-to-work" programme that would focus on young unemployed people, those who were long-term unemployed and out of work lone parents. The programme was to be funded by a one-off levy on privatized utility companies (Labour Party 1996).

This was part of a wider trend in a number of countries towards "activation" or active labour market policies (ALMPs). ALMPs are policies focused on moving people into, or closer to, the paid labour market, as opposed to "passive" policies that simply provide an out-of-work income. These policies can take various forms and can include combinations of different activities such as job searching assistance, work experience and training. These interventions are often underpinned by benefit "conditionality" – this means that citizens must engage with the support offered in order to receive out-of-work benefits (Clasen & Clegg 2011). The idea was that people disconnected from the labour market would be supported to return to work, increasing their income and welfare, reducing the fiscal costs of unemployment, and increasing labour supply.

In the UK, the former Department of Social Security and the Employment Service were merged into a new government agency, Jobcentre Plus. New services under the "New Deal" programme provided work-focused interviews for claimants in which advisors would run through "better-off calculations" and support people with childcare options, subsidized work placements, and voluntary work experience. These came alongside measures intended to "make work pay". A statutory minimum wage was introduced for the first time and changes were made to the benefit system with the introduction of Working Families Tax Credit and later Child and Working Tax Credit. Tax Credits were a system of cash support that topped up the earnings of working households on a low-income.

Although the focus was on support, and increasing the incentives to work in the design of the benefit system, this increased support also came with conditionality to participate. People claiming unemployment benefits were required, after an initial "gateway" period, to take up basic skills education, a voluntary sector placement, or a subsidized work placement (Van Reenen 2003).

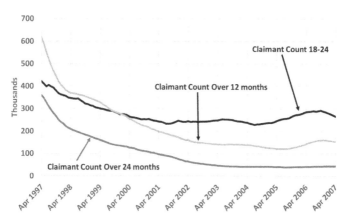

Figure 4.1   Youth and long-term unemployment, 1997–2007

Source: ONS time series AGNA, ADMD, AGMZ.

The following few years saw large falls in long-term unemployment and a significant fall in youth unemployment (see Figure 4.1). Several studies attempted to disentangle how much of this success was due to the broader economic situation and how much was down to government policy. John van Reenen (2003) found that rates of entry into work were significantly higher among unemployed young people in quarters 2 to 4 in 1998 (after introduction of the New Deal for Young People compared to the first quarter of 1997 (before the policy).

Whereas the measures targeted at youth and long-term unemployment were compulsory for claimants, voluntary New Deal programmes were also introduced for lone parents and disabled people, but with very different results. The lone parent employment rate rose by ten percentage points in this period (ONS 2021d). Mike Brewer and Andrew Shepherd (2004) surveyed a number of studies looking at the effects of policy during this period on parents' employment and concluded that the policy was partially responsible for the improvement in lone parent employment, and particularly for those with young children. On the other hand, the New Deal for Disabled People had very low take-up of 3.1 per cent and, although it helped those people who participated in the programme (Stafford *et al.* 2007), the low take-up meant it could not make a significant difference on its own to employment levels for disabled people.

By around 2004, the focus of the DWP had moved on to how to increase employment among those termed the "hardest to help". It was around this point that the DWP began its Pathways to Work pilot which sought to provide intensive active labour market support to disabled people (Becker *et al.* 2010). However, with the Global Financial Crisis at the end of 2007 bringing with it the most severe peacetime recession since the 1930s, the focus switched back to the unemployed.

FUNDING

Active labour market policies do not come cheap. It is far less costly simply to get a claimant to tick a box and sign a form to say they've been looking for work then it is to call them in for interviews in which childcare options are discussed, potential vacancies identified and benefit calculators used to carry out "better-off" calculations. Not only does the contact with claimants take time but staff have to be trained in how to carry out more supportive and intensive engagements and provided with the knowledge to be able to offer useful advice to claimants.

The initial costs of welfare-to-work programmes were met by a £5.2 billion windfall tax on privatized utility companies, promised in the Labour Party's 1997 election manifesto. As a result, DWP resource budgets increased by 30 per cent in real terms in the five years to 2003 (see Figure 4.2). By this point, many of the reductions in unemployment had been achieved (see Figure 4.1), and the focus of the DWP had turned to those it termed the "hardest to help" – often those not on the unemployment rolls but on "inactive" benefits such as disabled people on Incapacity Benefit (DWP 2007). The Pathways to Work pilot from October 2003 aimed to test the most effective ways of supporting Incapacity Benefit claimants into work (Becker *et al.* 2010).

For the first seven years of the Labour government, all of the Secretaries of State at the DWP and its predecessor, the Department of Social Security, had been from the "Brownite" wing of the Labour government – more closely associated with the Chancellor of the Exchequer, Gordon Brown. In 2004 came the first in a succession of DWP Secretaries of State more closely aligned with Tony Blair (Waugh 2004), some of whom were more inclined to explore marketization of public services.

With the focus of active labour market policies switching to a smaller group of people, expenditure began to be reduced. One of the vehicles for this was outsourcing support for the unemployed,

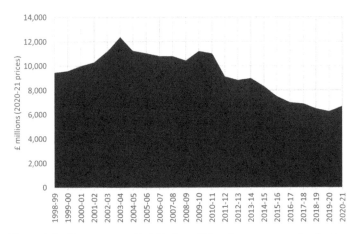

Figure 4.2 Department for Work and Pensions resource budget
in real terms

Source: Authors' calculations using HM Treasury, Public Expenditure
Statistical Analyses 2003–05, 2007, 2010, 2013, 2017, 2021.

whilst the state concentrated on the hardest to help groups. By
2008, plans were well under way for contracting out support for
the unemployed on a payment by results basis (DWP 2008). However, the Global Financial Crisis put paid to these plans. With
Gordon Brown as prime minister by this point, the focus of the
DWP shifted back towards tackling unemployment and most of
the cuts in expenditure since 2003 were reversed to cope with the
higher workload for the DWP during the ensuing recession.

UNIVERSAL CREDIT AND A DECADE
OF WELFARE REFORM

In 2010, the Conservatives came to power in coalition with the
Liberal Democrats on a manifesto that advocated no substantial redesign of benefits. Proposals on welfare focused mainly on

replacing Labour's welfare-to-work policies (Conservative Party 2010). However, eight months before the election, Conservative backbencher Iain Duncan Smith had been the driving force behind a report, *Dynamic Benefits:Towards Welfare that Works*, which had sketched out replacing many parts of the benefit system with two new benefits: one for in-work claimants and one for those out of work (Centre for Social Justice 2009).

Walking into the DWP as the new Secretary of State following the post-election coalition negotiations, he met senior civil servants who were armed with plans prepared under the previous Labour administration for a "single working age benefit" (Sainsbury & Weston 2010). In the face of the recession, and concerns about a scheme that would either produce substantial numbers of losers, or prove very costly, the Labour plans had not progressed to firm proposals (Timmins 2016). Within two months, the DWP had published a consultation and then, by November 2010, a white paper setting out plans for what the DWP billed as the "most significant change to the welfare system since the Beveridge reforms in 1947": the introduction of Universal Credit (DWP 2010: 46). The new benefit, as it is being delivered does the following:

- *Merges benefits into one*: Universal Credit pools all out-of-work means-tested benefits, in-work tax credits and Housing Benefit, into one payment.

- *Increases automation of benefit processing*: interaction with claimants is "digital by default" through an app rather than by attending a job centre; benefit calculation is based on monthly "real-time information" reporting of pay by employers to HMRC.

- *Includes in-work claimants within the scope of benefit conditionality*: they can be required to seek additional work

– either more hours or higher pay as a condition of receiving in-work benefits.

These changes occurred alongside three crucial changes to active labour market policies and benefit conditionality, which could have been implemented without the above changes to benefit design and delivery, and were therefore not strictly dependant on Universal Credit. However, they are nevertheless often presented as part of the same package: (1) *Intensified conditionality*: increased participation conditionality and increased behavioural conditionality; (2) *Greater sanctioning*: higher likelihood of sanctions, more severe penalties, imposed for longer periods of time; and (3) *Reduced expenditure on support*: reductions in support budgets, firstly through the Work Programme, and then through the Work and Health Programme.

Much has been written about the problems with delivering the new benefit: two of the clearest accounts are reports by the National Audit Office (NAO) in September 2013 (NAO 2013) and the Institute for Government in 2016 (Timmins 2016). Universal Credit has been slowly rolled out over the past decade and is currently scheduled to be fully implemented by 2024. At the time of writing (2022) most people making new claims for financial support due to being out of work or on a low income will now receive Universal Credit. For those already in receipt of the previous "legacy" benefits including Jobseeker's Allowance and Tax Credit, a programme of "managed migration" began in July 2019 to move people across to Universal Credit, although this was suspended due to the Covid-19 pandemic.

AN ARCHETYPAL "WORK FIRST" REGIME

The UK's approach to ALMP has evolved over time. As we have shown above, while the emphasis, approach and funding deployed on UK ALMP has varied over the years, successive governments have placed increasing emphasis on conditionality for unemployed people, expanding this to different groups in the labour market including lone parents and disabled people. Today the UK is now widely recognized as an archetypal "work first" welfare regime. The work first approach emphasizes fast work (re-)entry underpinned by requirements to make a high number of job applications. Here, looking for a job should be a full-time job in itself, and any job is considered better than no job. Considerations of job quality are sidelined.

So, for different UK governments, moving people into work and reducing social security spending has been the main goal – but this has tended to mean any work. Policies tend to be evaluated in relation to the proportion of people who find and stay in work. Little attention has been paid to the nature and quality of jobs people move into. As we discuss later in more detail, even as Universal Credit extends conditionality to working claimants, the quality of jobs people are required to apply for and engage in still seems like an afterthought.

5

Employment policies today

Is the UK's current approach effective in helping people back into work? Or could it be that the focus on "work first" actually gets in the way of achieving a "higher pay, lower welfare" economy? To answer these questions, we need to explore in more detail the focus on moving people into any job, the role of sanctions and low benefit levels and the employment support offered to people looking for work.

Universal Credit is now the primary vehicle for active labour market policy (ALMP) in the UK. It is both an in- and out-of-work benefit – underpinned by conditionality alongside financial sanctions if behavioural expectations are not met, but also employment support from Jobcentres and other employment support providers. Universal Credit extends and intensifies the conditionality for out-of-work social security claimants that has increasingly featured in UK active labour market policy over the past few decades. People claiming out-of-work benefits and subject to conditionality must meet UK government prescribed requirements including: attending appointments at the job centre, completing online jobseeker journals, providing evidence that they are actively seeking work (typically looking for work 35 hours per week), or participating in training or welfare-to-work programmes (e.g. the Work Programme).

Failure to meet the conditions attached to their benefit may

result in a "benefit sanction" – meaning that a person's benefits are reduced or suspended. In an unprecedented move, and
because Universal Credit is also an in-work benefit (see Chapter 2)
conditionality may also be applied to working claimants – so people who are working may now face new expectations to increase
their hours or pay in exchange for additional income through
Universal Credit.[1] In the UK, Jobcentre Plus – the Public Employment Service – and within them work coaches, are the first port
of call for those seeking work. However, contracted providers
increasingly feature – as non-state organizations deliver various
welfare-to-work programmes (e.g. the Work Programme, Work
and Health Programme and most recently Restart).

ANY JOB IS BETTER THAN NO JOB: IS WORK FIRST A PRODUCTIVE APPROACH?

Now considered an archetypal work first regime, the UK's approach focuses on moving jobseekers into work quickly. As we
showed in the previous chapter, over time, the UK's approach has
become increasingly directive, requiring jobseekers to accept any
job offer. Those claiming out-of-work benefits must sign a Claimant Commitment, which outlines their responsibilities in relation
to finding paid work. They must undertake intensive job seeking
and engage with various other work-related activities including
work-focused interviews at Jobcentres in exchange for low levels
of social security payments.[2] Here, any job is considered better
than no job; policymakers sideline considerations of job quality
and ensuring that jobs are well-suited to people's skill sets and
capabilities.

---

1 For in-work families, Universal Credit replaces Tax Credits, which did
not come with work search requirements.

2 See OECD (2022) for an international comparison of unemployment
benefits.

But is this the right approach? Policymakers justify their focus on fast work entry with reference to the evidence that engaging in paid work is good for both people and the wider economy (Freud 2007). They also point to record high levels of employment as proof that this approach is working – although the employment impact of Universal Credit prior to the Covid-19 pandemic is "highly uncertain" (Work and Pensions Committee 2018). Notably, they have been less keen to claim credit for the growth in poor quality employment and poor productivity performance that has lain underneath strong headline measures.

Scant attention has been paid (in policy debates or academic research) to understanding how recent welfare reforms that intensify and extend conditionality interact with and impact on the labour market, including productivity-related issues. However, some researchers have begun to draw links between the UK's poor productivity performance, its "long tail" of low-paid and insecure work, and a welfare system which curtails the choice and bargaining power of unemployed and low-income workers (Innes 2018; Rubery *et al.* 2018).

While the work first approach may be effective at moving some people into employment in the short term, there are questions over its longer-term outcomes, and the extent to which this approach to ALMP is effective at supporting the whole population. International evidence shows that although sanctions-backed conditionality can make work entry more likely in the short term, in the long run it results in lower wages and increasing flows into economic inactivity (NAO 2016).

While most research has focused on short-term employment outcomes, recent research conducted by Henri Haapanala (2021: 360) which compares the impacts of different ALMP approaches across countries to involuntary part-time employment found that coercive, 'hard' ALMP instruments incentivizing rapid re-employment with the threat of withdrawing unemployment benefits are associated with higher likelihood of involuntary part-time employment, whereas supportive, 'soft' ALMP strategies with a focus on upskilling and public sector occupation are associated with higher voluntary but lower involuntary part-time employment.

They conclude that by "applying hard activation instruments to achieve full employment, an unintended consequence might be the expansion of precarious employment".

Thinking about the UK's approach to ALMP and whether it supports or undermines the Good Work agenda, it is helpful to consider two key issues. The first is about the question of fit, and whether or not this approach moves people into the right jobs. Supporting people into the jobs that are a good match for them is key to sustained job outcomes (Sissons & Green 2017). But does the UK's work first approach support people to apply for jobs that are appropriate to their skill sets, or if they are off the claimant count do we not care where they end up? Are we helping people to find suitable jobs that are possible to manage alongside caring responsibilities and health problems?

The short answer is no. Research has repeatedly highlighted shortcomings of the work first approach in relation to sustained job outcomes. Through large-scale qualitative longitudinal research with social security claimants, The Welfare Conditionality project, for example, found that the UK's work first approach failed to support sustained transitions into meaningful work (Dwyer *et al*. forthcoming).

A requirement to take any job risks inhibiting good matches by pushing people towards jobs that they are not well suited to. This can make work search efforts futile for those who are required to apply for jobs that they are neither suited nor qualified for, undermining their prospects of, and confidence about, moving into work. Those who do take up jobs to which they are not well-matched can struggle to sustain them: "I'm a builder; I've been in the building trade 40 years and he wanted me to apply for administration in a library ... anybody would laugh at you, wouldn't they? ... I don't think I'd be able to do the job and I don't think any manager or supervisor would've employed me ... that's a bit silly really, isn't it?" (male, aged 55, claiming Universal Credit, cited in Jones 2019).

A second, and related, issue is about power. It is employers – not unemployed people or low-paid workers – who have ultimate power over the quantity and quality of work on offer (Osterman 2013). Through enforcing a requirement to take any job through the benefits system, the state shapes people's power in the labour market. Claimants are not only required to look for a high volume of jobs, but they may also face a sanction if they voluntarily leave their job (i.e. if they quit) or reduce their pay.

Employer demand for flexible labour in the form of zero-hours, agency worker, or other piecemeal employment contracts is met when claimants are required to take on any job. There is little incentive for employers to make work good, if they know they will always be able to recruit people to poor quality roles. So, by focusing solely on short-term increases in the employment rate and short-term reductions in the claimant count, the state arguably works to undermine the bargaining power of individuals, reinforcing one-sided flexibility as workers are required to be available for and take any job in order to reduce their dependency on the welfare system. Research conducted by Kendra Briken and Phil Taylor (2018) on the experiences of people working in an Amazon warehouse provides a stark illustration of this power dynamic by demonstrating how low-paid insecure workers can feel trapped between a punitive welfare system and exploitative employers: "I did not have any choice. I had to take the job there and then or I would have had my benefits stopped ... although the job is horrible, the pay is poor, there's always pressure because mostly you can't meet your targets, I will be applying to work there again in November because you have to have a job or your benefits get stopped" (worker quoted in Briken & Taylor 2018).

So, we can see how the UK's general approach to tackling unemployment not only ignores, but also potentially undermines the decent work agenda by funnelling unemployed people into low quality jobs with few prospects to escape the no-pay-low-pay cycle.

CRUEL TO BE KIND? THE DISEMPOWERING
IMPACT OF SANCTIONS AND DESTITUTION

The requirement to take any job is backed up by financial sanctions. Alongside the introduction of Universal Credit, the past decade of welfare reform has seen the intensification of a sanctions-backed conditionality regime – as the volume, length and severity of sanctions have ramped up considerably. In 2012, the possibility of a three-year sanction was introduced (Adler 2018). This was followed by what David Webster (2018) has termed the "great sanctions drive". This is illustrated in Figure 5.1, which shows the total number of sanctions referred each month to decision-makers[3] since April 2000, and clearly demonstrates a steep rise to a peak of more than 200,000 in 2013/14. Analysis from the NAO (2016) found that roughly a quarter of people claiming between 2010 and 2015 received at least one sanction.

---

3 Sanctions are referred to a DWP decision-maker when a front-line adviser believes that the claimant has breached the conditions of their benefit. Although it varies by benefit, around half of these sanction referrals are upheld by decision-makers. Since 2016, the DWP has failed to publish statistics on the total number of sanction referrals where Universal Credit has been fully rolled out (full service) – only those whose sanction referral is confirmed by the decision-maker. So, we have estimated the number of rejected referrals based on the average rate at which referrals have been confirmed in recent years.

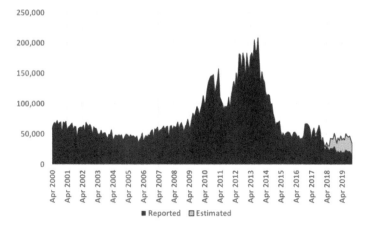

Figure 5.1 Total number of sanctions referred each month to decision-makers

Source: DWP Stat-Xplore, DWP Benefit Sanctions Statistics and authors' calculations.

A combination of sanctions, low benefit levels induced via successive caps, cuts and freezes and the five-week wait for a first benefit payment have resulted in severe financial hardship. In part as a result of this approach, 2.4 million people in the UK are estimated to be experiencing destitution (Fitzpatrick *et al*. 2020). This means they are unable to afford at least two of five of the essentials they need to eat, stay warm and dry, and keep clean.

Some justify sanctions-backed conditionality regimes in paternalistic terms – a "cruel to be kind" approach which will encourage people to move away from poverty and welfare "dependency". This, it is argued, is ultimately in the long-term interests of individuals (Watts *et al*. 2014). Similarly, restricting entitlement and maintaining low benefit levels are also justified in this way. So, what does the evidence say about whether this is an effective way to support people into work?

Although some quantitative studies have found that in the

short term, sanctions can be effective at reducing the claimant count, studies focused on employment outcomes paint a mixed picture. In the longer term benefit sanctioning has been found to result in reductions in earnings and employment duration (Grogger & Karoly 2005; Griggs & Evans 2010).

Sanctions are counterproductive for a number of reasons. First, there is a very practical issue in that financial sanctions can actually prevent people from looking for work as they are unable to cover the costs of doing so: "The sanctions, I think, have held me back from being able to go and look for work ... I wasn't able to get out and look for work further away, but if I wasn't sanctioned I would've been able to look for work in [nearby city]" (Universal Credit recipient, welfare conditionality project; see Dwyer *et al.* 2018).

Second, the threat of sanctions can shift the focus of social security claimants towards meeting the conditions of their benefit claim in order to avoid sanctions-induced destitution, rather than engaging in activities that might productively lead to them gaining and sustaining employment. People must engage in pointless activities (e.g. applying for jobs for which they are not qualified or well-suited) in order to avoid sanction, rather than enhance their prospects in the job market.

This is illustrated by the experience of a Jobseeker's Allowance claimant who had previously served in the armed forces. Interviewed as part of a study led by Lisa Scullion exploring veterans' experiences of the UK welfare system, he described going through the motions of Jobcentre requirements even though he felt more specialized routes into employment were more appropriate:

> [I spend] Every day logging on to Universal Jobmatch, which to me isn't appropriate for me because there's a lot of recruitment companies out there that do ex-Forces, which is better for me. So Universal Jobmatch is a bit of a pain in the backside, because sometimes you log on to

apply for a job just so it covers you to show them in the Jobcentre you've been looking for work ... You have to log on to Universal Jobmatch even though it's no good to you (ex-Forces JSA claimant, in Scullion *et al.* 2019).

Described by one Conservative MP as a "military-style command and control approach" (Alston 2018), this approach has meant that claimants need to spend time jumping through the hoops of the welfare system rather than engaging in more meaningful activities that could help them move into work: "I don't give them an inch. I don't give them any opportunity to say you've not done this we're going to sanction you. I cover my back thoroughly" (benefit recipient with two children, cited in Andersen 2020).

So, while a familiar mantra is that looking for work should be a full-time job in itself – in reality, satisfying the demands of the social security system uses up much of that time. These are not the productive and "socially valuable" activities those advocating such work-centric approaches had in mind (Patrick 2012). In addition to not helping the people in question, it is also not welcomed by employers, who complain about the costs of dealing with a deluge of inappropriate applications. As one social care employer reflected when interviewed by one of the authors (Katy Jones) in 2019: "We get people applying for jobs just so they can sign on and say that, 'Look, I've applied and I've been for interviews', and then waste all our time because they don't actually want the job ... It's a cost to our business" (social care provider, in Jones *et al.* 2019).

Thirdly, and perhaps most significantly given the importance of good health to a strong and productive economy, is that the impact of sanctions-based welfare conditionality on health and well-being can be devastating. Dwyer *et al.* (2020) for example, found through qualitative longitudinal research with 207 UK benefit recipients, that instead of helping people to move into or closer to the paid labour market, conditionality triggered negative health outcomes making future employment less likely: "It felt like there might even be more sanctions in the pipeline. I just went into meltdown for several weeks actually where I couldn't function ... All I could think of was the enormity of the struggle, to get out of this nightmare, get the sanction overturned, appeal the sanction, deal with the fresh threat of sanctions" (benefit claimant cited in Dwyer *et al.* 2020).

Quantitative research conducted by Evan Williams (2021), in which he used quarterly panel data for local authorities in England and fixed effects models, has shown that sanctions led to increases in anxiety and depression amongst social security claimants. Looking at low benefit levels, Aaron Reeves and colleagues (2022) estimate that "the prevalence of depression or anxiety among those at risk" of being subject to the 2016 benefit cap increased by 2.6 percentage points "compared with those at a low risk of being capped".

Somewhat ironically, policymakers' fixation on tackling "idleness" has also created rather a lot of work for others. A report published by the National Audit Office in 2016 found that not only do sanctions have disastrous consequences for individuals, they also represent a "high opportunity cost ... for the efficient use of public resources". Additional costs borne by other agencies such as debt advice agencies, charities, housing providers and healthcare professionals because of the Universal Credit rollout are substantial (Bennett 2017a). These agencies put a tremendous amount of effort and resources into dealing with the fallout from the five-week wait that new claimants must endure, low benefit payments, sanctions, and the adverse impact the welfare system can have on people's mental health. Charities and other third sector organizations have had to shift from providing more meaningful activities – employment support and training, and other activities related to health and well-being – to dealing with the fall-out: "Crisis work ... has become a priority ... the number of people in situations where they've been going for week after week without money ... that kind of work has taken a priority over the last year or so" (homelessness charity worker, cited in Jones 2021).

Food bank use has rocketed. In 2010/11 the Trussell Trust's network of food banks distributed 61,000 emergency food parcels, by 2019/20 this had risen to 1.9 million. The Trussell Trust has identified insufficient income provided by the UK's social security safety net as the most significant driver of food bank use. However, it is also striking to note that among those needing to draw on this vital source of support, 1 in 7 live in a household where someone is in work (Trussell Trust 2021).

IS THE TIDE TURNING?

The UK's sanctioning regime has softened slightly in more recent years. Sanction rates have been reducing, and under the stewardship of Amber Rudd while Secretary of State for Work and Pensions, the three-year sanction was removed. In 2019, acknowledging some of the counterproductive impacts highlighted above, she announced: "I will end financial sanctions for welfare claimants that last for 3 years ... I believe they were counterproductive and ultimately undermine our goal of supporting people into work". However, the general principle of intensive job search backed up by the threat of sanctions remains. Sanctions are still a key element of the government's approach to moving people into work – and the threat for individuals looms large.

The devastating financial impact of low benefit levels more generally also continues to be dismissed by policymakers. While in 2020 Universal Credit was increased by £20 per week, this was only a temporary measure introduced as part of the government's response to the Covid-19 pandemic. Moreover, even with this uplift, there was a striking contrast between the generosity of the furlough scheme where median earners have been able to keep 80 per cent of previous wages compared to what could be received through the benefits system.

Ignoring evidence and protests from charities, academics, and MPs including many of those from his own party and key Universal Credit architect Iain Duncan Smith, Prime Minister Boris Johnson defended the decision to remove the £20 uplift from Universal Credit:

> *Stephen Timms*: If the cut goes ahead in three months' time, unemployment support will be at its lowest level in real terms for over 30 years ... According to the Joseph Rowntree Foundation, half a million people would be pushed below the poverty line by taking the £20 away, including 200,000 children, and the universal credit allowance for under-25s, who have obviously been hard hit by job losses in the pandemic, will be cut by a quarter. Can all that damage really be justified?

> *Boris Johnson*: I think that the best way forward is to get people into higher wage, higher skilled jobs ... if you ask me to make a choice between more welfare or better, higher paid jobs, I am going to go for better, higher paid jobs. (HoC Liaison Committee, Oral evidence from the Prime Minister, HC 491, 7 July 2021)

But no-one was asking him to make a choice between more welfare and better jobs. As this chapter has shown, inadequate social protection for those outside of work can undermine the objective of people getting into better jobs.

SUPPORTING PEOPLE INTO WORK: EMPOWERING PUBLIC EMPLOYMENT SERVICES?

Sanctions clearly have disempowering effects. But active labour market policy isn't just about job search expectations and sanctions – even in Work First welfare systems. The flipside of the conditionality coin is *support* to move back into work. Here, when people find themselves out of work, the government has an opportunity to help them (re-)enter the labour market and potentially even strengthen their position. Alongside encouragement, it could provide tangible careers advice, and support to access childcare, transport and training opportunities, which could ultimately strengthen people's position in the labour market.

Unfortunately, employment support appears to have fallen some way down the agenda. A Claimant Commitment outlines what individuals must do rather than how the state can support them, and the system appears to be centred on an objective to make life difficult for people rather than help them. As a policy official quoted in Lord Freud's (2021) account of his time as a DWP minister put it: "Basically it's a great big nagging service".

We explore in more detail in later chapters the support provided to particular groups, alongside support to access skills and support progression. However, overall, research focused on the experiences of claimants suggests this is limited and bears little resemblance to the more enabling, person-centred approaches to "employability" more common in educational settings (Whelan *et al*. 2021). Fletcher and Wright (2018) characterize it as a "DIY", "bargain basement" approach.

Jobcentres now focus mostly on processing and monitoring compliance with Claimant Commitments and disciplining those who fail to meet the expectations set by their work coaches. An emphasis on fast entry into any job, combined with assessment, surveillance and enforcement has warped the objectives of a system which could be about supporting people into sustainable work. Frontline workers focus on moving people off benefits (which does not necessarily mean a move into work, education, or training).

Although cross-country comparisons should always be made with caution, given differences in monitoring and reporting, it is helpful to look at how we fare in relation to our competitors. As demonstrated in Figure 5.2, despite increases in investment in the early 1990s as part of New Labour's New Deal programmes, UK investment in ALMPs remained well below that of other countries.[4] The data is only shown for 2011, as the UK appears to have stopped providing statistics after this date.

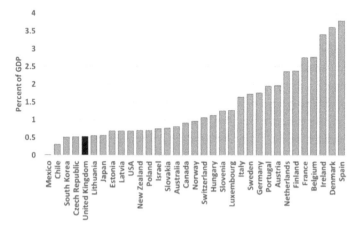

Figure 5.2   Total public spending on labour markets, percentage of GDP, 2011

Source: OECD.

More recent figures shown in the previous chapter demonstrate significant retrenchment of the public employment service (Jobcentre Plus) and funding for other contracted providers as part of government's package of austerity measures, limiting the support claimants could receive. There is little in the way of rights to support and services – and the support someone receives can hinge on the discretionary judgements of work coaches. While more staff were drafted in to deal with the sharp rise in Universal

4 See https://data.oecd.org/socialexp/public-spending-on-labour-markets.htm for the OECD definition of public spending on labour markets.

Credit claims following the first UK Covid-19 lockdown, over time our public employment services have been neglected and starved of investment.

As has also been a common feature in other welfare states such as Australia, UK welfare-to-work provision is increasingly outsourced, and contracted non-state providers feature in the provision of employment support, particularly for those who are long-term unemployed (Kaufman 2020). Programmes for the long-term unemployed (formerly the Work Programme, now Work and Health Programme and a new Restart programme), are delivered by a range of private providers on a payment by results basis.

The Work Programme was also commissioned on a "black box" basis, which meant that employment providers were able to design and deliver whatever they felt was appropriate to move the claimants they were working with into work (Bennett 2017b). Providers received different levels of payment, according to the different "group" claimants were allocated to (depending on prior benefit type) and the extent to which their job outcomes were sustained. However, despite an emphasis on sustained job outcomes under the Work Programme, the general approach appears unchanged. The black box and differential payment structures did not appear to lead to the innovations forecast by its architects. As one Universal Credit claimant describes:

> They farm you out, basically. You still go and sign on at the Jobcentre, but you're farmed out to [Work Programme provider] who are supposed to help you find a job. The operative word there is 'supposed'. They don't give you any help . . . Well, you turn up, and they just say, 'What jobs have you applied for?' So you show them, exactly the same as you show when you go to sign on, it's exactly the same . . . You just turn up and it's almost as if it's another signing on (claimant, cited in Jones 2019).

Instead, the shift to payment by results models has resulted in the widespread practice of "creaming and parking" – the concentration of support by providers on those already nearest to the labour market, and the exclusion of people with more complex and difficult barriers. Those with more significant hurdles to labour market entry were often sidelined and left without support (Carter & Whitworth 2015).

Sanctions-backed conditionality with minimal support is particularly ineffective for those with more significant barriers to work. In a recent review of the evidence base, the Institute for Employment Studies concluded that "programmes that prioritize support over conditionality appear important for vulnerable groups" (Newton *et al*. 2020). A combination of individualized support and training combined with trusted relationships with advisors helped people to build confidence and encouraged movements towards or into work.

Overall, too much "nagging" rather than help can make people reluctant to engage with a system that should be there to help them back into work and access social security payments they are entitled to. It is estimated that approximately 480,000 young people don't claim the benefits they are entitled to, which in turn makes them ineligible for support from such programmes as sector-based work academies and Kickstart which form part of the UK ALMP landscape (Jones *et al*. 2018).

There is also a disconnect between employment support and broader industrial and macroeconomic strategies. To date there's been no real attempt to link up people who need work to quality jobs in key growth sectors. While a small amount of sector-focused activity can be observed through initiatives like sector-based work academies for young people, a general requirement to look for and take any job is a missed opportunity to build up capacity in the sectors we want – and need – to grow in.

The UK urgently needs to shift its economic structure (for example, a shift to green jobs) and there are skills shortages in key sectors (such as social care and construction). At the time of writing, HGV drivers were one of many labour shortages faced by the UK economy. If we had spent the last decade focused on training and skills rather than sanctions, we might not have gotten in such a mess: "An HGV driver right, I had to apply for that but I don't drive. Now where's the logic there?" (male Universal Credit recipient, welfare conditionality project).

A lack of support for older workers in particular can mean they are left without adequate support to retrain and switch to growing sectors as some industries decline.

PARALLEL POLICYMAKING: WELFARE-TO-WORK AND THE GOOD WORK AGENDA

The last decade of welfare reform has played out at the same time as the Good Work agenda has grown in prominence in UK policymaking and debate. However, despite a shared focus on work, there is a clear disconnect between welfare reforms focused on tackling unemployment and supporting low-income workers, and broader employment policy.

Universal Credit was considered a policy area too "complex" and outside the remit of the Taylor Review of modern working practices, other than to say that a "more dynamic, responsive welfare system" was a good idea in principle (Taylor 2017: 99). The report completely ignored issues relating to conditionality. As a policy with implications for several employment and productivity-related issues, this omission is striking. ALMP is clearly a policy area with implications for the supply of labour, workplace social dynamics, management practices, skill development and worker well-being, all of which impact on productivity (Jones 2021).

We can also observe the absence of job quality considerations in more targeted programmes, where the state has more control to shape the nature of job opportunities ALMP participants are

able to access. A recent example of this can be seen through the
Kickstart job creation programme, which was introduced to stem
predicted increases in youth unemployment as a result of the
Covid-19 pandemic. Announcing the Kickstart scheme in his Plan
for Jobs speech, Chancellor Rishi Sunak emphasized that participants "need to be doing decent work". However, equating this
with jobs of 25 hours per week paid at the minimum wage seems
a very low bar. Beyond this rhetoric, there is little evidence that
the quality of these opportunities was a consideration.

There will no doubt be good examples where employers
offered high quality jobs through this scheme – but this will have
been through luck rather than policy design. However, this is an
example where a clear policy is needed. This was clearly a missed
opportunity to influence the quality of jobs available to young
unemployed people rather than just playing lip service to the
decent work agenda.

The development of UK ALMP has occurred in isolation from
"good work" debates and the underlying approach of the DWP
continues to neglect the issue of job quality. Furthermore, despite
the fact that the government's ambition for a "higher pay, lower
welfare society" forms a key part of its productivity plan (HM
Treasury 2015b), not much attention has been paid to claims that
it will help to "improve productivity". As other parts of government are beginning to think about "Good Work", the DWP has
remained fixated on moving unemployed people into any work
quickly – this was even at a time of record employment. The development of "in-work conditionality" has appeared to involve much
of the same thinking – with suggestions of a "work first, then work
more" approach.

WHAT NEEDS TO CHANGE?

There is another way. Human capital development approaches
to ALMP, more common in Scandinavian countries (for example

Sweden), adopt more enabling strategies, treating periods out of work as an opportunity to support people to develop their skills and equip them for a changing labour market (see Lindsay *et al.* 2007; Heins & Bennett 2018; Whelan *et al.* 2021 for more detailed discussion of these approaches). These policies place greater emphasis on improving skills and connecting people with high quality training and employment. Researchers have for a long time lamented the limitations of the UK's work first approach, but now more than ever it appears ill-equipped to respond to the challenge of low pay and productivity – and ultimately its unambitious approach to providing public employment services. Especially given policymakers' focus on good work and productivity, we need a shift in focus towards good jobs not any jobs, emphasizing sustained job outcomes with opportunities for progression.

The intensity of job search requirements should be reduced to give unemployed people more choice and an opportunity to focus on producing good quality applications welcomed by employers rather than a high quantity to satisfy state requirements. "Decent work" expectations in job creation programmes should be clearly set out and monitored.

The status of what should be considered a vital public service also needs to be elevated. Enhancing meaningful support from work coaches should be a priority – we need a qualified, motivated and well-resourced public employment service that is shaped by claimant support needs and barriers to work. Policymakers need to recognize and deal with the disempowering – rather than motivating – effects of benefit sanctions. Reducing their severity is paramount and they should be repositioned as a last resort rather than a constant threat pervading employment support. We need a support-based rather than a sanctions-based system.

6

Employment gaps

They didn't really talk about that [caring responsibilities] to me much but I don't think they really care about that. They made me feel as though I just needed to get back to work. They didn't really care about how I would find child-care for training or how it would affect my children.

Mother of two children
(cited in Andersen 2020)

Today's workforce is much more diverse than 80 years ago. However, there is still much further to go. Ethnicity, disability and gender employment gaps are endemic in the UK labour market. The gap between the employment rates of lone parents and the general population, for example, is amongst the largest in Europe (Romei & Conboye 2019). Analysis from the Trades Union Congress (TUC 2020) shows that disabled people had an employment rate of 54 per cent, compared to 82 per cent for non-disabled people. High levels of "hidden unemployment" among those with disabilities and long-term health conditions represent the exclusion of many disabled people from work (Beatty & Fothergill 2005). Women, young people and other disadvantaged groups are being hardest hit by the economic fall-out induced by the Covid-19 pandemic (Evans & Dromey 2020).

Certain demographic groups including women and disabled

people are also over-represented in poor quality, low-paid work. In 2020 disabled workers earned £2.10 an hour (19.6 per cent) less than non-disabled workers (TUC 2020). This is due in part to the greater likelihood of both lone parents and disabled people to work part-time, in the case of mothers typically due to the need to balance work with caring responsibilities (Ray *et al*. 2014).

In the UK there is a significant part-time pay penalty that is not observed to the same extent everywhere. Here, part-time workers are concentrated in lower paid manual, elementary and service occupations, whereas in countries such as Germany and the Netherlands, part-time work is more available across the occupational structure, with a higher proportion of better pay-ing part-time roles (Warren 2008). This has been argued to result from relatively weak regulation in the UK, which does not have as much protection for short-time workers compared to other countries (Ray *et al*. 2014). Tackling gender pay gaps has moved up the agenda in recent years, with the introduction of mandatory reporting. The TUC and others are now calling for ethnicity pay gap reporting.

Supporting the labour market participation of excluded and marginalized groups should be a core focus for policymakers. However, existing welfare-to-work models do not always suit those with more difficult and complex barriers to work. As high-lighted in the preceding chapter, ALMP outcomes are often poorer for people with more significant barriers to labour market participation.

In this chapter we explore this issue further drawing upon the recent experiences of two groups – lone parents and disabled peo-ple – who are increasingly the target of mandatory participation in active labour market programmes via the UK social security system. What is clear is that a generic one-size-fits-all employ-ment service is not fit for purpose and that pushing people into any job can further undermine their power in the labour market, reducing their prospects for future progression.

Citing low employment rates, policymakers have targeted groups like lone parents and disabled people for "activation". Consequently, not only has conditionality intensified, but its reach has also extended to groups who were previously exempt (Dwyer & Wright 2014). However, the government's existing approach has had very poor outcomes for particular groups. The government-funded Work Programme, for example, performed particularly poorly for lone parents and disabled people (only 2.6 per cent and 2.3 per cent respectively moved into employment during the first 14 months) (Whitworth & Griggs 2013).

LONE PARENTS

The New Deal for Lone Parents (NDLP) introduced in 1998 was the first major government programme to target employment support at lone parents in the UK. Operating alongside a suite of other New Deal Programmes, NDLP provided information, referrals and financial support, and was introduced at the same time as broader measures to "make work pay" including more generous in-work support through the Working Family Tax Credit (WFTC), support for childcare and the National Minimum Wage in 1999. Positive employment outcomes from the (voluntary) NDLP have been attributed to the flexible and tailored support it provided (Hasluck & Green 2007).

However, the engagement of lone parents in such programmes and broader work search requirements has become increasingly mandatory. Since 2001, lone parents claiming benefits were required to attend work-focused interviews (mandatory from 2004), and in 2008, Lone Parent Obligations (LPOs) were introduced, which in effect moved lone parents onto the main unemployment benefit (Jobseeker's Allowance), requiring claimants to engage in job-seeking and take up paid work (Lindsay *et al.* 2018). At that time, lone parents were subject to work search requirements when their youngest child was aged 12; however, this age has since been repeatedly lowered – from 2017 to pre-school children as young as three under Universal Credit.

While there are some "flexibilities" for lone parents claiming out-of-work benefits, which allow them to restrict working hours in line with the age of their child and other circumstances, these too have been restricted over time. Failure to look for work and meet Jobcentre requirements puts lone parents and their families at risk of a financial sanction, bringing them in line with the treatment of other jobseekers (Johnsen & Blenkinsopp 2018; Lindsay *et al.* 2018).

This increasingly mandatory approach has been justified by policymakers who point to larger impacts of mandatory support on employment rates than observed with the voluntary New Deal. An evaluation of the LPO reform found that this led to an increase in the share of lone parents in employment between 8 and 20 percentage points. However, this only tells part of the story. A later survey conducted with LPO participants found that two in five working households remained in material deprivation. The introduction of LPOs was also estimated to have increased the proportion of lone parents who were out of work and not claiming benefits (see Ray *et al.* 2014 for a detailed summary of this evidence).

Looking beyond the numbers, the picture painted by qualitative research with lone parents is not a positive one. Research exploring their experience of support from Jobcentres has found this to be variable, and often negative (Lindsay *et al.* 2018). Although some lone parents have positive experiences and encounter work coaches who are "understanding, caring and respectful", this does not appear to be widespread. Jobcentre staff are more typically described as "unsympathetic, judgemental and/or patronising" (Johnsen & Blenkinsopp 2018).

Research with lone parents claiming Universal Credit by the charity Gingerbread, found that Jobcentre staff were not felt to understand their needs. Many did not even have a named work coach. This results in generic requirements to search for work, rather than realistic expectations that take into account personal circumstances and offer genuinely tailored provision (the tailored approach of the Making it Work programme outlined in Box 6.1 is a striking contrast). Lone parents report that they do not receive consistent information about the flexibilities available to them (such as how many hours they were expected to work or engage in job searching, and about access to wider support such as training and education).

Better experiences were reported where work coaches referred lone parents to specialist providers (Dewar & Clery 2020). However, support provided by more generic contracted services like the Work Programme, has been characterized as limited and focused mainly on job searching and applications (Lindsay *et al*. 2018). Unsurprisingly, lone parents have had poor job entry outcomes as a result.

Although many lone parents are motivated to engage in the paid labour market, they face significant personal and structural barriers to entering, sustaining and progressing in work (Johnsen & Blenkinsopp 2018; DWP 2021a). A lack of flexible and tailored support fails to meet their needs and the absence of affordable childcare remains a significant barrier to labour market inclusion. Finding suitable work that fits with childcare, transport and other commitments is incredibly difficult.

Although some support is provided to cover the costs of childcare under the new Universal Credit system, this is currently paid in arrears (parents are required to pay for this up front) and childcare provision that matches working hours can be difficult to secure. Timewise (2019) and other campaigning groups have highlighted a shortage of part-time flexible work that parents can fit around their caring responsibilities. Golden "middle of the day jobs" are difficult to find (Dewar & Clery 2020).

On top of this, limited access to adequate and affordable transport can make balancing work and care impossible (see Chapter

9). For those lone parents who do enter employment, it is typically characterized by low pay, insecurity and limited opportunity for progression (Lindsay *et al*. 2018). It is perhaps no surprise then that 33 per cent of children of working lone parents are living in poverty (Cribb *et al*. 2017).

DISABLED PEOPLE

Disabled people are also increasingly a focus for labour market "activation" and, like lone parents, have been brought under the remit of the UK's conditionality regime. Again, while disabled people's participation in ALMPs began on a voluntary basis (e.g. via New Labour's New Deal for Disabled People), over time, policy has become increasingly underpinned by compulsion (Etherington & Ingold 2012; Dwyer *et al*. 2020).

The Freud Report, commissioned by the Labour government in 2007, called for a move away from unconditional social security, advocating the extension of conditionality to *all* economically inactive groups (including disabled people). This informed the Welfare Reform Act 2007 which marked a step change in the government's approach to supporting disabled people who are not in work. Significantly, Incapacity Benefit, disability related Income Support and Severe Disablement Allowance were phased out. In their place a new benefit – Employment and Support Allowance (ESA) – was introduced from 2008 for those claiming out-of-work benefits on the grounds of disability or ill health. This new benefit was introduced alongside a new assessment process (the Work Capability Assessment, hereafter WCA) which would determine how much a person's ability to work is impacted by a disability or long-term health condition.

There were initially three main outcomes from the WCA. Those deemed "fit for work" were moved to Jobseeker's Allowance, and as such were required to engage in job-seeking and work-related activities in exchange for their benefit. A second group were found to have "limited capability for work" but were considered capable of work in the future. This group were placed in the work-related activity group. Here, claimants were expected to engage in work-related activities but conditionality is reduced compared to those on Jobseeker's Allowance. A third group, assessed as having as "limited capability for work and limited capability for work-related activity" were placed in the ESA support group. This group are not required to engage in work search or other work-related activities in exchange for their social security payments. Universal Credit has since replaced ESA, yet the WCA and approach to determining the extent to which someone is fit for work, and hence the conditionality regime they are subject to, remains broadly the same (DWP 2020).

Before we think about the adequacy of employment support for this group, it is important to acknowledge the many examples of poor experiences of the assessment and claims process. WCAs have been criticized for being a dehumanizing and humiliating process, with evidence and advice from claimants' doctors being overruled by WCA assessors (Garthwaite 2014; Ryan 2020; Scullion & Curchin 2022). Particular difficulties have emerged in relation to understanding and assessing mental health impairments and the support claimants experiencing these require (Scullion *et al.* 2019). They are widely considered a poor assessment of people's capability to work. Many WCAs are successfully appealed, yet while overturned, the ongoing uncertainty induced by this process creates considerable anxiety and distress (Dwyer *et al.* 2018): "I think you do get a lot of conditions where as a whole they present to you and using your medical knowledge in the background, you think 'you probably couldn't reasonably work for whatever reason', yet they don't score on any descriptors" (a WCA assessor, cited in Baumberg Geiger 2018).

Alongside these recent reforms, benefit levels for disabled people have been repeatedly cut, resulting in significant financial hardship. Disabled jobseekers are also much more likely to be subject to a benefit sanction than those with no disabilities/ health impairments. Analysis by Ben Baumberg Geiger (2018) found that disabled Job Seeker's Allowance claimants were 26–53 per cent *more* likely to be sanctioned than non-disabled JSA claimants. Benefit sanctions have had disastrous consequences for many disabled people, in many cases pushing them further away from work and in extreme cases have been linked to suicide (Reeves 2017; Merrick 2020).

In relation to employment support, as with lone parents, disabled people report a lack of tailored, "person-centred" support from both Jobcentres and contracted-out provision (Dwyer *et al*. 2018). Disabled people engaging with various contracted-out programmes including the Work Programme and subsequent Work and Health Programme, have had poor employment outcomes. In the rare instances they do receive it, disabled people value practical advice and support through policies such as the Access to Work scheme (a government scheme introduced in 1994 that offers practical and financial support to overcome work-related barriers resulting from a disability or health condition), which are found helpful to access employment.

But overall, a focus on fast work entry crowds out more meaningful support which might realistically help to empower and improve disabled people's position in the labour market. An overwhelming emphasis on policing benefit eligibility forces unhelpful distinctions between those deemed fit or unfit for work and a punitive approach to conditionality has been widely criticized as inappropriate for those with health needs. Particular issues have emerged for those with fluctuating conditions and mental health impairments. Analysis of 207 qualitative longitudinal interviews over a two-year period with out-of-work social security claimants reporting having some kind of mental health impairment found that all elements of their claim: assessment, benefit sanctions and requirements to engage with employment support were often experienced negatively. Conditionality applied to those claimants was largely ineffective in moving people into or closer to paid work. In fact, it actually triggered negative health outcomes, potentially making future employment less likely (Dwyer *et al.* 2020).

Payment-by-results models incentivize providers to centre efforts on supporting those closest to the labour market, sidelining those with more significant barriers, working to push "disabled jobseekers further away from paid employment, rather than towards workplace inclusion" (Scholz & Ingold 2021: 1604). Reflecting on his experience spending 18 months embedded in the DWP as a mental health specialist, Tom Pollard (2018: 9) concluded, "in contrast to the rhetoric of 'activating' people [Jobcentres and ALMP] actually promotes a cautious and unambitious approach to working with those with more complex needs and circumstances".

Although some disabled people cannot work due to physical and/or mental health conditions, many who are not in work do see engagement in the paid labour market as a goal either in the immediate or long term. However, while policymakers fixate on perceived attitudinal and behavioural barriers to work, a lack of tangible support combined with widespread discriminatory attitudes and practices can prevent many from realizing these goals.

Liz Sayce, visiting senior fellow at the London School of Economics and former chief executive of Disability Rights UK starkly highlights the imbalance and injustice of a system that focuses more on punishing disabled people than discriminatory employers:

Disabled people are over 60 times more likely than employers to face sanctions for non-compliance with requirements. In 2015/16, disabled people were sanctioned 69,570 times for missing appointments or infringing work-related conditions of benefit payment ... Employers in the same year were in effect 'sanctioned' only around

1,100 times when disability discrimination cases were either settled or won by a disabled person at Employment Tribunal. (Sayce 2018)

Perversely, it is often when disabled people are deemed *not* fit for work, and so are not subject to conditionality, that they are actually able to start thinking about and working towards paid work. As participants in the Welfare Conditionality project (2018) reflected:

> It's only really getting into the support group that gave me that freedom to focus on what I wanted to do and not to have to put all my energy into jumping through pointless hoops and cope with the stress and anxiety of not knowing whether I was going to be referred to sanctions every month ... It's really ruined people's lives. People have just lost that kind of foothold that they had in terms of taking part in society or maintaining an activity that enabled their wellbeing or gave them some hope for the future. That's just had to go out of the window because all their energy has gone in complying with stupid conditionality. (Disabled woman, welfare conditionality project)

> I had instant relief when I knew I was having well over a year without being sanctioned, that immediately helped me start thinking, right, work. (Disabled woman, welfare conditionality project).

The need for improving support for disabled people through the benefits system and employment services is widely recognized. A recent report from the Work and Pensions Committee (2021) on the disability employment gap exposed significant shortfalls, and the government is currently consulting via it's *Shaping Future Support* green paper (DWP 2021b) which focuses on support to "start, stay and succeed in work and ways we can improve the experience people have of the benefits system".

In addition to improving support, more promising approaches pay greater attention to the work opportunities available, rather than narrowly focusing on conditionality for disabled claimants. Disabled people responding to a recent Work and Pensions Committee inquiry highlight the technique of "job carving", whereby employers adapt or create roles to match the skills of an employee. This technique has also been identified by the Equality and Human Rights Commission as something that could improve employment outcomes for disabled people. Although the Committee notes that the DWP does encourage providers of some of its programmes to engage with employers to job-carve roles for participants, it recommends that it should do much more.

BOX 6.1 CASE STUDY: TACKLING LABOUR MARKET EXCLUSION: MAKING IT WORK, SCOTLAND

The Making it Work programme was funded by the Big Lottery Fund (2013–17) in five local government areas. It provided intensive personalized support for lone parents facing labour market exclusion. Lone parents engaged voluntarily with the scheme which aimed to support them to progress towards employment and achieve broader positive social outcomes. Of 3,115 participants, around 30 per cent entered employment.

Delivered by partnerships comprising public and third sector stakeholders, the programme offered personalized support provided by keyworkers embedded in local communities with small caseloads. Support was flexible, intensive, and sustained and included a range of service designed to support people to build confidence and financial capability, alongside pre-employment and vocational training. Participants were supported to access childcare and were signposted to other services focused on employability, learning and well-being. The programme did not rely on payment-by-results models increasingly utilized by national policymakers. Instead, flexible partnership memoranda and service level agreements enabled services to be flexible and responsive to service users' needs and aspirations. Shared grant funding based on consensus prevented unnecessary competition between partners to "claim" job entries, and guarded against the practice of "creaming and parking" which often features in payment-by-results models favoured by government.

> "I didn't really have that many high hopes, to be honest . . . but she [MIW keyworker] made me feel at ease straight away. There's like, no judgement whatsoever. She just wants to help you. And it was all about trying to build my confidence up and everything and speaking about what would be the best type of job for me. And what would fit me better and it was always, 'Don't go for something that you don't think would suit you. Do something that you know that you can do'." (Service user, Edinburgh, 2015)

Researchers have highlighted the inevitable limits to the programme, including a lack of good quality flexible labour market opportunities and inadequate childcare provision. However, central to the positive experience of participants appears to have been that it helped them to feel more "in control" despite this challenging backdrop. The evaluation team highlight the key differences between this person-centred approach and that of the mainstream employment support service: "lone parents engaging with the programme consistently spoke of a sense of empowerment and control over their employability journeys. Whereas many had previously felt pressured – and sometimes even intimidated or humiliated – when engaging with Jobcentre Plus and/or compulsory activation ... MIW encouraged participants to make choices about the services that they received, the pace of their progress towards paid employment, and the type of work or other activity that was to be their final destination" (Lindsay *et al.* 2018).

WHAT NEEDS TO CHANGE?

Active labour market policies for lone parents and disabled people have been designed around the assumption that behavioural and attitudinal barriers are the central drivers of low employment rates amongst these groups. Instead of creating support and services that meaningfully seek to address the disadvantages that they face in the labour market (i.e. childcare, transport, work adaptations), or creating the conditions whereby good quality jobs are accessible to those seeking part-time work, the government has focused on processing and policing benefit entitlement. Fixation on the "behaviour" and "attitudes" of claimants combines with the absence of tangible support. Instead of designing policy and services to support and empower people in the labour market, UK ALMP can make life more difficult for many.

The underlying problem is a "one-size-fits all" approach as a way of delivering cost savings in welfare-to-work programmes. The outsourcing of employment programmes to large private sector providers on a payment-by-results basis has led, inevitably, to widespread "creaming and parking", which we mentioned in the previous chapter (Carter & Whitworth 2015). In recent years, further cost savings have led to welfare-to-work programmes being scaled back even further (e.g. Work and Health programme).

As new welfare-to-work programmes are introduced, it is vital that these work for groups with the biggest barriers to work.

However, while investment in supply-side measures – through improving the employment support available – is important, it can only take us so far. The Making it Work Scotland case study (see Box 6.1) shows that even where support is provided that meets participants' needs, there are limits to any intervention within a labour market characterized by low-paid low-quality work. Much more needs to be done to make work better and fairer for groups who continue to be excluded, including lone parents and disabled people.

7

Supporting low-paid workers

Universal Credit transforms the way the state interacts with workers on a low income. Alongside more stringent requirements for out-of-work claimants to engage in job-seeking activity, it may – controversially – involve the introduction of "in-work conditionality" to claimants on a low income, placing responsibilities on individual workers to increase their earnings.

The traditional distinctions drawn by policymakers between strivers and skivers, workers or shirkers, are now blurred as both unemployed people and low-income workers come under the DWP's remit. But the big question is *how* will this change the way the state interacts with people in work? In this chapter, we focus on how the government might support this group. After briefly outlining this policy shift, we review recent developments in this new, experimental, policy area and consider whether or not we are on the right track not only to support people into, but also to progress in work.

IN-WORK BENEFITS:
FROM TAX CREDITS TO UNIVERSAL CREDIT

Alongside conditionality for people who are out of work, many countries also seek to incentivize employment via in-work benefits. As with active labour market policies (ALMPs) for the unemployed, in-work benefits also vary in design. They are also typically combined with other "make work pay" measures including minimum wages, and have the twin aims of incentivizing employment and reducing in-work poverty (Clegg 2015). Particularly since the 1990s, and against a backdrop of "deindustrialization and labour market flexibilization", in-work benefits saw considerable expansion across advanced welfare states – as the carrots to the sticks of conditionality (Clasen 2020: 2).

In-work benefits have made a significant difference to the incomes of low-income working households (Ray *et al.* 2014). They have also been historically popular across political divides. However, while they are "a response to . . . the growth of low-wage jobs and atypical types of employment", they may also support it (Clasen 2020: 10). Policymakers express concerns about both the sustainability of growing in-work benefit expenditure, and the extent to which it subsidizes part-time and/or poor quality work (Clegg 2015).

The UK has been a keen innovator of policymaking in this area as it explores the possibility of extending behavioural conditionality to working social security claimants. The Social Security Advisory Committee (SSAC 2017) described this as a "ground-breaking" move with "no comparable precedents", and marks a fundamental shift in the reach of conditionality to those in work. It will no longer be enough to be in work – work must in future meet the requirements of the DWP's conditionality regime.

This has important implications for those receiving in-work benefits, who have varying needs and circumstances both within and outside the paid labour market. Pre-Covid, it was estimated that approximately one million households could be subject to in-work conditionality once Universal Credit was fully rolled out (SSAC 2017). The exact parameters of this policy are still being worked through. However early trialling is indicative of a "work first, then work more" approach. Below we consider who the new "in-work" cohort is, we reflect on findings from initial government randomized control trials before considering more recent advice to government from the In-Work Progression Commission.

WHO ARE WORKING UNIVERSAL CREDIT CLAIMANTS?

Research commissioned by the DWP and published in 2021 (DWP 2021a) provides detail on the characteristics of the "future cohort" of working Universal Credit claimants who may fall under an "in-work conditionality" regime. This is the group who are currently claiming tax credits and housing benefit, who, until now, have not had to engage with DWP in-work services. The majority are women (77 per cent) and most are parents (70 per cent), while 15 per cent care for another adult. Half are lone parents (51 per cent), a fifth (20 per cent) are couples with children, and the remainder (30 per cent) are single people or couples without children.

The average age of claimants in this cohort is 45 and more than a quarter (27 per cent) report that their daily activities are limited due to a health condition or disability. Just less than a fifth (18 per cent) are from an ethnic minority. Their qualification levels are varied – 14 per cent have no qualifications, whereas 17 per cent are educated to degree level or above – however most commonly claimants hold level 2 (GCSE at grade A*–C or 4–9) and level 3 (equivalent to A level) qualifications. Three quarters of the cohort report that they are struggling financially, despite the regular top up for income provided by the legacy tax benefit system.

In terms of the paid work they are already engaging in: this group are working an average of 21 hours a week and most have been in their current job for over a year – 41 per cent have been in their current job for over 5 years. Most have a permanent contract (77 per cent), however some are on zero-hours contracts (16 per cent) or work on a temporary or seasonal basis (4 per cent). Job satisfaction is high amongst this cohort – with 81 per cent satisfied with their job overall. For a majority (64 per cent), keeping their current job is their main priority. Many are unable to progress in work due to the need to balance work alongside caring responsibilities and health conditions – as has been found in wider research (see Kumar *et al.* 2014; Ussher 2016), responsibilities like this restrict the jobs available to this group.

> I think in the restaurant business, if you want to progress you've got to be able to drop your life. Well, within a big company anyway ... While you're training they might send you to Leeds one day, or they might send you down to London the next day. You can't really have a life while you're doing it, you can't have children or anything. (Young woman, Sheffield, cited in Ussher 2016)

Parents within this group emphasize the importance of stability within their current work role – they are reluctant to make changes at work due to the potential disruption this could have on managing caring arrangements and responsibilities alongside work. Nevertheless, 72 per cent of participants in the DWP commissioned research reported taking steps to try and progress at work, for example, by undertaking training or asking managers about progression opportunities. Increasing their pay is a priority, rather than increasing hours or getting new jobs. There is a reluctance to trade their current stability for higher paid posts with more variable hours and less security.

Although a majority (74 per cent) report feeling confident that they could find progression opportunities, or could apply for a new job (63 per cent), almost half (47 per cent) felt they needed to improve their skills and qualifications first. For older claimants and those who had been in the same job for a long time, outdated IT skills made them less confident about applying for jobs with progression opportunities. This group of claimants are also pessimistic about the availability of opportunities to progress in their local labour market – 61 per cent think that the jobs available don't pay enough to make working more hours worthwhile, and just over half think that there aren't enough full-time vacancies for everyone.

People in work claiming Universal Credit will clearly be a very varied group, with different support needs and preferences. The researchers commissioned by the DWP segment the new cohort into different groups: the "keen to progress" (17 per cent); "motivated but cautious" (33 per cent); "care-focused" (22 per cent); "stable but stuck" (12 per cent); and "stable and content" (16 per cent). While in varying positions, all place a high value on being in work that fits with caring responsibilities and/or health conditions and 50 per cent want to be in a role that pays enough for them to come off benefits completely. This is *before* the DWP intervenes and in-work conditionality is applied. What this demonstrates is that conditionality will make little difference to people's motivation to progress – that is already there. Many want to work more but this is difficult for a number of reasons, including the need to balance work and care, and a lack of full-time jobs with stability. The support required to progress varies according to individual circumstances, however priorities include support with childcare, debt and skills training. The researchers conclude that tailored support adapted to varying circumstances and requirements is needed.

WORK FIRST, WORK MORE:
THE SHAPE OF THINGS TO COME?

Even though the exact parameters are yet to be pinned down, early stage trials and official guidance suggests the government's approach to in-work interventions appears remarkably similar to their out-of-work approach – so a "work first, then work more" approach: "one-to-one support from a Work Coach, coupled with increased conditionality, may encourage individuals in the same way that it does for those out of work" (DWP 2018b: 20).

Guidance for employers (DWP 2018a), for example, states that workers on a low income who are in receipt of Universal Credit, may be expected to either: (1) increase their hours; (2) look for ways to progress in their current workplace; (3) search for additional work with a different employer (i.e. take on multiple jobs); or (4) take up alternative work elsewhere (i.e. move jobs). Much in the same way as the long-established drill for out-of-work claimants, these expectations may be backed up by support from the Jobcentre (for example, through advice from work coaches), but also by penalties (benefit sanctions) if individuals do not comply with mandatory work-related requirements.

While framed positively in terms of progression (this is the DWP's "In-work Progression" policy), early trials of in-work interventions have worryingly continued to emphasize the quantity rather than the quality of work and genuine progression (DWP 2018b). The DWP's approach to date appears narrowly focused on increasing the numbers of hours worked (Wright & Dwyer 2021), rather than more common definitions centred on higher pay or more holistic conceptualizations of progression which incorporate greater stability and security, and scope for longer term career development.

Perhaps unsurprisingly then, the government's own trialling of in-work conditionality does not suggest it is effective in engendering meaningful progression. A randomized control trial (DWP 2018b) in which different levels of conditionality were tested did not find evidence of a statistically significant impact on earnings 15 months after starting the trial. The DWP's own impact assessment found a small significant impact – with participants in a "frequent support" group earning an average of just over £5 more per week. The frequent support group participants had fortnightly Work Search Review (WSR) meetings with Jobcentre work coaches and job search actions agreed as part of the trial were mandatory.

The commissioned researchers highlighted the importance

of tailored and practical support rather than other measures, like the frequency of meetings, was more important in supporting progression. However, work coaches involved in the trial reported high variation in terms of the extent to which they had been trained on how to support people in work, and their confidence in doing so. This appears to have impacted on the level of support provided – whereas some were using meetings to have meaningful conversation about career aspirations, others were simply reviewing actions in Claimant Commitments. The DWP appear ill-equipped to develop support that is not centred around what claimants can be made to do through compulsion.

The 5-year ESRC-funded Welfare Conditionality Project, which also interviewed Universal Credit claimants subject to in-work conditionality, found that they struggled to meet expectations to attend appointments at the Jobcentre where these clashed with work shifts and childcare arrangements: "I'm still getting letters and being called into [Jobcentre] on Friday … Even though they know I'm in work … It's one of those … compulsory ones again, and if I don't attend it I'll probably end up in trouble … [S]o I won't be able to work on Friday again" (working UC claimant, cited in Wright & Dwyer 2021). This was especially challenging for those in jobs with variable hours: "Since I've been doing this UC it's so much worse: [I]f you work for 20 hours a week in a job you've still got to do another 15 hours searching to make your wages up. Yes, I can work full-time if the work is there but there are zero-hour contracts where I don't know if I'm working until the day before" (working UC claimant, in Wright & Dwyer 2021).

The impact of in-work conditionality will depend on factors like how it is applied, and how claimants and – crucially – employers respond. However, there has been very little consultation with those likely to be affected by this policy change to understand how it is likely to affect their working lives. The DWP's "test and learn" approach does not appear to be one developed with those whom it affects.

Understanding how employers might react is a key gap here. Katy Jones (one of the authors) recently interviewed employers about how they might respond if their employees in receipt of Universal Credit were subject to in-work conditionality (see Jones 2022). Although some felt it could help to encourage staff to try to progress in work, they voiced concern that simply increasing hours worked would not be productive for their business, and that the policy might lead to increased staff turnover and higher recruitment costs.

Employers were critical of high volumes of (often unsuitable) applications generated by an existing "work first" approach – and they felt this would be exacerbated by extending conditionality to working claimants. Several reflected that the policy could also impact negatively on their relationships with their staff, should tensions emerge from a mismatch between their requirements and those of the Jobcentre. However, ultimately, they felt that they would be unlikely to change their business practices. Hiring staff on a flexible basis is central to many business models. As one hotel manager explained: "We wouldn't want to have every single person on a full-time contract. We'd still need some flexibility to fluctuate with the demands of business levels" (employer, cited in Jones *et al.* 2019).

Rigid expectations to work a 35-hour week are therefore clearly at odds with the reality of low-paid work. But while potentially creating significant problems for businesses, the real people in the crossfire of in-work conditionality policy are the individual workers – caught between what may be conflicting demands of the work coach and employer, required to engage in a never-ending search for something that is neither desirable nor attainable. Employers also wield significant control over the lives of workers who don't have the power to leave them. When asked about how they might respond to requests from their staff to take on jobs with other employers to boost their earnings, some employers said they may prevent workers from taking up additional work through "conflict of interest" clauses: "If some-one who works in reservations upstairs or sales upstairs comes to me with this proposition of going to the next-door hotel, then unfortunately, there is a contractual clause that will bar them from doing such a thing" (employer, hotel, cited in Jones *et al.* 2019).

Alongside particular implications for those (mainly women) who are combining work and caring responsibilities, there is a real danger that this policy will result in a more transient workforce, wherein more and more people juggle multiple jobs. Universal Credit encourages the take up of small hours work – as claim-ants do not have to meet various thresholds to be eligible, as was the case with the tax credit system. So there is a danger that this results in people moving into poorer quality bite-size jobs with less attachment to employers who have even less incentive to invest in the skills of these staff, especially if they are taking on multiple jobs.

It also raises the question of future entitlement to social secur-ity and pensions. Auto-enrolment – automatic enrolment into employer-provided pension schemes – and building up of en-titlement to contributory benefits are both subject to minimum earnings thresholds. People who divide their working hours between separate roles with small numbers of hours in each are more likely to fall beneath these thresholds and fail to build up entitlements.

A MORE SUPPORTIVE APPROACH?

Although the development and implementation of in-work interventions appears to have paused – perhaps delayed by the emergency response needed to support new Universal Credit claimants as a result of the Covid-19 pandemic – now is a good opportunity to reflect on whether or not a work first, work more approach is the right one going forward.

In 2021, a DWP-commissioned review, led by Baroness Ruby McGregor-Smith, focused on supporting progression out of low pay. While somewhat dodging the issue of conditionality and sanctions (it is scarcely mentioned), the McGregor-Smith Review advocates supportive, incentive-based approaches: "The Commission understands the sensitivities around sanctions and would like, instead, to propose a system of incentives". The review also highlights, as we do in this book, the importance of ensuring other aspects of government policy – notably skills, transport and childcare align to support rather than frustrate this agenda.

Does the McGregor-Smith Review signal a welcome shift in the DWP's approach? The current Secretary of State for Work and Pensions Thérèse Coffey commits little at this stage other than to "consider it carefully", so we are yet to see.

In-work support *could* be helpful – if it is meaningful, appropriate and sensitively delivered. It is a challenge to reach and support low-paid workers and Universal Credit offers a mechanism to do this. However, more of the same – a work first, then work more approach – is not only unambitious and unfair: it risks undermining wider government priorities to shift to a higher wage, higher productivity economy.

Furthermore, while the In-work Progression Commission provides a welcome shift in tone, a focus on in-work progression should arguably be adopted from the outset – rather than as an added extra: "UC seeks to strengthen incentives to enter any paid work, and amongst those who are already in work, to increase hours or earnings" (DWP 2017). An emphasis on progression is something that should be factored into the approach to move people into work in the first place. A "work first, then work more" model is no good, but a "work first, then we'll support you to progress" model is also misguided as we know progression from poor quality jobs is difficult.

BEYOND CONDITIONALITY: IS UNIVERSAL
CREDIT WORKING FOR WORKING PEOPLE?

Although our analysis has focused on conditionality, the design of Universal Credit more generally has been found wanting in terms of adequately supporting those in work. Policy ideas seem to have been developed in the abstract, based on assumptions about the way the labour market works (assumptions of civil servants and policymakers in well-paid, stable jobs with career progression) and the way work is managed within households.

While perhaps logical within the walls of Whitehall, its design clashes with several features of the UK labour market. For example, the decision to pay Universal Credit monthly is sup-posedly in order to "mimic" the paid labour market when in fact at the bottom end of the income distribution, a lot of workers are paid more frequently. Analysis from the Resolution Foundation, for example, found that "the majority (58 per cent) of new claim-ants moving onto UC as a result of moving from employment were paid either fortnightly or weekly in their previous job" (Brewer *et al.* 2017). For the average household, a monthly payment may seem sensible, but this system has clearly not been designed for those on lower incomes, and in more precarious forms of work, who are more likely to be paid at the end of the week or shift.

The DWP uses automated data feeds from employers and a strict monthly assessment period to decide the next month's Universal Credit payment. This sounds like a reasonable process but the reality is that adjusting automatically to a person's pay on this basis can mean that some are hit with significant deductions from their Universal Credit payments if they are paid twice within one assessment period (as can happen with early Christmas paydays), or if they receive a bonus. Managing an income which is both tight and variable is incredibly difficult and Universal Credit's monthly assessment period – alongside the new risk of being sanctioned while in work – can exacerbate volatility in income amongst those who are already struggling.

Furthermore, as Jane Millar and Fran Bennett point out (2017: 171), while "the claimant commitment makes clear that welfare is no different from work itself", "the contract imposed by Universal Credit carries very heavy sanctions and penalties, much more stringent than what might be expected in an employment contract". Most workers might have occasionally been late for work, but few face a swingeing deduction in pay extending for some weeks if this happens.

The generosity of Universal Credit has also been in the spotlight recently with the decision to remove in October 2021 a temporary increase of £20 per week attracting widespread criticism. As it was first designed, Universal Credit offered a mixed picture in terms of generosity with some groups likely to gain from the new benefit and some to lose out (Alakeson *et al.* 2015). But the benefit we have today is very much the poor relation of that designed originally by Iain Duncan Smith. There have been a series of cuts that have progressively reduced its value, starting with George Osborne's Summer Budget of 2015. Working-age benefit rates were frozen for four years. Cuts to the benefit cap hit people particularly hard in high-cost housing areas, and the two-child limit broke a long-established principle that the state would not punish the child for the so-called "sins" of the parent.

One measure that was specifically targeted at in-work claimants was large reductions in work allowances – the amount that low-paid claimants could earn before benefits started to be withdrawn. The July 2015 Budget originally included making similar cuts to tax credits – the in-work predecessor of Universal Credit – but these were so unpopular that they were reversed in the Autumn Statement in November that year. However, the Universal Credit Work Allowance reduction was left in place. Effectively, this became a slow-burn cut that would take effect gradually as more people made the transition from tax credits to the new benefit.

Since then, there have been some ameliorations: there was a small increase in work allowances in 2018 and in 2021, a reduction in the Universal Credit taper from 63 per cent to 55 per cent and further increases in work allowances. For higher earning in-work families with children or a disabled adult, these changes mitigated the removal of the £20 uplift but out-of-work claimants, those without children, and families with children earning less than the equivalent of around 30 hours of work at the minimum wage are still likely to be worse off.[1]

In 2022 and 2023, the focus will once again be on the sufficiency of benefit rates as post-pandemic supply chain disruption and high energy prices cause a jump in prices throughout the economy. Each April, benefits are usually increased in line with the previous September's inflation.[2] On this basis, benefits rose in April 2022 by 3.1 per cent. However, the OBR's forecast was that prices in 2022/23 would be 8 per cent higher than in the previous year (OBR 2022). This shortfall between annual Consumer Price Inflation growth in September and CPI growth in the following tax year is the largest ever seen.[3] The result is that benefits are estimated to fall by 5 per cent in real terms in 2022/23.

---

1 Authors' calculations. Families with children with no housing costs working less than 28 hours a week at the minimum wage are likely to be worse off. Those with housing costs are likely to be worse off if working less than 34 hours a week at the minimum wage.

2 George Osborne's benefit freeze from 2016 to 2019 is the only period in several decades when there was no April increase. Benefits for non-disabled working-age claimants were held at their 2015/16 levels until April 2020.

3 Authors' calculations using ONS time series D7BT and D7G7, and the OBR's March 2022 Economic and Fiscal Outlook.

WHAT NEEDS TO CHANGE?

If government wants to support workers to progress out of low pay, it is critical that we move away from the work first approach for those *outside* of work. Poor quality, insecure work acts as a trap rather than a stepping stone to better quality work. Under the work first regime, people move into poor quality jobs with limited progression because they are required to do so. Why not focus on supporting people into the *right* job, which fits with their capabilities and aspirations and offers scope for further progression? This is key to better outcomes from ALMP and underlines arguments made in the previous chapter about the need to adopt wider notions of employability, incorporating opportunities for lifelong learning and giving people the power to turn down poor quality jobs.

If the DWP does want to shift its emphasis towards higher quality work and higher wages, this must translate into practice on the ground. We should not underestimate the scale of change required: there will need to be a fundamental change in DWP policies, practices, and the way it measures the success of its active labour market policies. For example, it is important that the DWP's performance management and performance indicator regime reflects the value of job entry at higher wage rates (or the potential for these). Statistical information on the success or otherwise of its activities must include measures that capture the effectiveness of job matching and entry into jobs with potential for progression. Crucially, short-term benefits to annually managed expenditure (AME) resulting from the emphasis on entry into any job, and increasing hours, must be balanced against the contribution to longer-term productivity of faster progression for low-paid workers and better health and well-being, as well as reductions in longer-term fiscal expenditure.

It is also important for policymakers to recognize and be realistic about the power and choice individuals have in the paid labour market. A large part of the problem lies with the demand side, i.e. the availability of work opportunities and their quality, and yet a "work first, then work more" approach locates this firmly with the individual – the actor with arguably least power over the quality and quantity of work they do.

Yes, in-work benefits like Universal Credit can be seen to subsidize low-paid and poor-quality work, where part-time work is involuntary and paid work isn't providing people with enough to meet a basic standard of living. However, it should also be recognized that some want and need to work part-time (albeit there is a need for more quality and better paid part-time work).

But although UK policymakers boast about having one of the most flexible economies in the world, there is a risk that this policy shift will punish low-paid workers for it. We do need to improve the quality of jobs, but we also need a safety net that adequately supports people who are running the gauntlet of low-paid insecure work at the sharp end of the labour market. For Boris Johnson to justify recent cuts to Universal Credit on the basis that we need to move towards a higher pay economy unfairly puts the blame for low pay at the feet of low-paid people. Both unemployed and low-income workers are now framed as the new idle. But if the government are serious about moving towards a high-pay, high-productivity economy, their focus should be on employers rather than subliminally communicating this intent via the hardship of people in poverty. As an employer interviewed in Katy Jones's recent study clearly puts it: "It would be probably more beneficial for the government to help employers become better employers, and to make the workplace a more positive environment than it is to push employees to get more jobs" (employer, soft play centre, cited in Jones *et al.* 2019).

8

Skills and progression

They keep trying to send you on the same courses . . . You're like, 'Mate, we've done all that' . . . They've got a checklist of about 14, 15 courses, and they're all pretty badly taught anyway . . . A one-day health and safety course; they will string it out for two weeks.

Universal Credit claimant,
sanctions, support and service
leavers project (Scullion *et al.* 2019)

The UK has a skills problem, but it is not a straightforward one. On the one hand, we have an oversupply of skills. According to the 2011 British Workplace Employment Relations Survey (WERS), 19 per cent of respondents felt their skills were "much higher" and 33 per cent "a bit higher" than those required by their job (Sutherland 2013). The absence of good quality part-time jobs we highlighted earlier means that women in particular are often trapped in jobs for which they are overqualified. For example, a survey carried out in 2015 found that 52 per cent of retail workers feel overqualified for the work they do (Ussher 2016).

Recent research from academics at King's College London and Working Families (2021) has shown that a need to compromise on finding work that better aligns with people's skillsets, qualification levels and capabilities in order to access part-time/flexible jobs that allow them to fit around caring and other non-work needs means that many workers are trapped in low pay despite being highly skilled. People working in jobs where their skills are not being used earn less and have fewer opportunities for progression. They also have lower well-being, motivation and job satisfaction compared to workers with skills that are valued and put to use (Boxall *et al*. 2019).

There is also a problem with undervaluing people's skills. In some low-pay sectors such as social care, it is not the case that skills are being underused – rather, that they are undervalued. UK care workers are amongst the lowest paid in Western Europe, and the scale of underpayment across the sector means that many care workers are denied even minimum entitlements (Gardiner 2015). Recent legal battles for equal pay in retail, where certain roles, more likely to be carried out by women, have been undervalued compared to others, also show that undervaluing of skills is a common experience for many low-paid workers (Butler 2021). The common thread across these examples is of course gender: it is feminized sectors (such as social care) and feminized roles (such as shopfloor assistants) where undervaluing is more likely.

However, despite underutilizing and undervaluing existing skills, the UK also has a problem with shortages of skills in certain areas. The UK performs poorly in terms of basic, intermediate and technical skills levels (Abreu 2020). This makes it all the more concerning that adult learning participation has declined considerably over the past decade, following a period in which the adult skills budget has been slashed. Analysis by the Institute for Fiscal Studies shows that in 2020, total spending on adult education had fallen by two-thirds since 2003/04 (Britton *et al*. 2020). Analysis published by Aveek Bhattacharya and colleagues in 2020 shows that since 2004 adult education participation rates have almost halved from 29 per cent to just below 15 per cent.

Familiar pronouncements about the need for a "German style vocational education system" predictably resurfaced in response to concerns about pandemic-induced mass youth unemployment. But despite reform after reform, many of those who don't pursue academic pathways continue to be let down. Whereas other countries have invested considerably in vocational education and training, in the UK this often still lacks parity of esteem with academic pathways.

A limited focus on basic skills and general education in apprenticeships limits their role in helping people to develop the core skills they need to help them navigate a rapidly changing labour market and society (Boeren 2019). Furthermore, already set at low rates, one in five apprentices earn less than their legal entitlement (Low Pay Commission 2020). Although offering worthwhile opportunities for some, there are therefore concerns that more unscrupulous employers use the apprenticeship system to reduce their wage costs.

This is especially important to address today. Investment in skills is pro-cyclical – it is higher when the economy is doing better (Green 2021) – and there is a danger that skills inequalities may grow as businesses shift resources away from training and development in their attempts to weather the Covid-induced economic crisis. Although the concern about widening educational inequalities as a result of the pandemic have understandably centred on school-age children and young people in post-compulsory education, stark inequalities in access to adult education endure and the risk that these might widen is something we need to be much more concerned about.

EMPLOYER-LED TRAINING

Ensuring that people are able to develop the skills demanded by employers is important to ensure that individuals can access opportunities in the paid labour market, the competitiveness and growth of firms, and the economy more widely. Complaints from employers about skills shortages, particularly in sectors like health and social work, and construction and manufacturing have prompted attempts to involve them more in the development of education and training provision (DfE 2020).

Employer-led, employer-ownership and "putting employers in the driving seat" have all become familiar soundbites in the world of UK skills policy. There are some good examples of this working positively. Burgess and Vignoles, for example, credit employer involvement in apprenticeships with making these qualifications more valuable than other vocational options (Burgess & Vignoles 2020; Green 2021).

However, more generally employers fail to deliver the training that the economy and our society needs. Although investing in skills, training and development is considered a key part of being a "good employer", UK employers typically do not see it as their responsibility to invest in the skills and training of their workforce, preferring to "recruit rather than train" (Green 2021): "We do offer cross-training in other areas, but people generally are expected to do that in their own time . . . on your day off, you can go and spend a day on reception and try and find out how it works. They won't have been paid to do that because we need them to work their job that they're doing" (employer, hospitality sector, cited in Jones *et al.* 2019).

Workplace learning in the UK occupies a precarious position and has declined significantly over the past few decades. Training days per employee fell in almost all sectors between 2011 and 2017 (Green 2021). According to a recent Employer Skills Survey, one third of staff received no training in the past 12 months (Bhattacharya *et al.* 2020). The casualization of work reduces employers' commitments to their staff, reducing investment in skills and personal development. Business models tend not to involve a skills offer, especially for low-paid part-time staff. The lack of opportunities to develop and apply their skills means that progression opportunities in work are seriously limited. Where managers do invest in training, this tends to be job-specific rather than in broader skills needs such as literacy and numeracy. A tendency to focus on the day-to-day business of a firm can make workplace learning programmes difficult to establish and maintain (Wolf & Evans 2011).

Much of the solution to low skills utilization lies in better management and job design (Sissons & Jones 2016; Atkinson *et al*. 2019). Crucially, we need more higher quality part-time jobs which enable women in particular to balance work and care, without the need for compromise due to a lack of flexibility in higher paid roles. Declining employer investment in skills also requires urgent attention, as does a lack of clear pathways to support progression within firms. Offering better quality work, after all, will mean employers won't need to be quite so worried about losing the staff they invest in.

A ROLE FOR THE STATE

In some ways, the inadequacy of training provided by UK employers is unsurprising. Employers are not required to support workers to develop their skills. Economists point to a so-called "free-rider" issue, whereby employers are concerned that the investments they make in their workforce will benefit other firms if staff leave and take their newly acquired skills elsewhere. Why would employers support their workers to develop their skills, especially when it may ultimately equip their staff with the skills and/or qualifications they need to move on to better quality, higher paid jobs?

It is also the case that training and education provides "public goods" – benefits to society at large – over and above the benefit to the current employer. There is a benefit to the economy and society as a whole from having a better-trained workforce, over and above the private benefit to the employer from the higher level of skills. As a result, employers taking into account their own interests will never provide as much training as society needs.

Given that training suffers from two types of market failure – the free-rider problem and the public goods issue – it would represent the triumph of hope over experience to expect employers on their own to solve the UK's skills problems. These market failures demonstrate the need for a greater level of state intervention if the UK is to maximize its competitive position in the global economy. We know that investing in skills brings significant economic and social benefits (Lane & Conlon 2016; Abreu 2020). Skills are not only important for productivity, but also for tackling social and economic inequalities. Lifelong learning is critical if adults are to be able to adapt to rapid economic change and technological developments.

SKILLS AND UNEMPLOYMENT/LOW PAY

The UK's skills challenges are also important to consider in relation to unemployment and low pay. Firstly, it is important that the skills people have are matched to the jobs they do to prevent the high level of skills underutilization highlighted above. This supports further our arguments against the "work first" approach discussed in previous chapters. Requiring people to take any job regardless of whether or not it complements their qualification level and broader skill sets – whilst perhaps resulting in short-term cost savings through reduced benefit payments – comes at a considerable cost in the long term. It is better for both individuals and the economy if we focus on a better match between skills and jobs.

Secondly, particularly given the absence of employer investment in skills, the state should be playing a key role in supporting people who are unemployed and on a low income to access opportunities to develop their skills. We know that learning participation is particularly low amongst adults who are unemployed and in low-paid, insecure work, and that both unemployment and working in low-skilled jobs result in skills atrophy – as a person's skills deteriorate when not in use (Reder 2009; Bound *et al*. 2018).

Despite the issues highlighted above regarding skills under-utilization, gaining new skills and qualifications are still often key for progression to higher paid, better quality jobs, and can help people retrain and move into better jobs and higher paying sectors (Sissons 2020). The extension of working lives, economic restructuring and technological change also mean that opportunities to re-skill are imperative, but older adults and those with jobs most at risk from automation are also less likely to engage in learning (Abreu 2020).

However, a need for individuals to bear the cost of learning participation rather than the state, and a lack of support especially for those pursuing non-higher education courses combined with uncertain returns in a polarized and fragmented labour market means that adult learning is disincentivized (James & Boeren 2019). Training and skills should therefore be a central component of efforts to support people into good quality work, particularly if it means that workers are empowered to access better quality jobs.

Crucially, the government needs to ensure there is a skills offer that is not dependent on current employers, and it should also play a more active role in encouraging adults to take up learning opportunities. One way it could do this is through its interactions with unemployed and low-income workers via Universal Credit. This is what we focus on in the remainder of the chapter.

SUPPORTING LEARNING THROUGH THE WELFARE SYSTEM

The welfare system *could* open up pathways into education and training for unemployed and low-paid workers. Through Universal Credit, there is an opportunity to reach precisely those groups who are excluded from good quality training opportunities.

Recent research has neglected to explore in much detail the training and educational content of support for Universal Credit and other benefit claimants. But as we noted earlier, studies exploring more generally support for jobseekers have highlighted a lack of tangible support and a narrow range of training options. Our public employment services have been characterized as having a "DIY/bargain basement" approach (Fletcher & Wright 2018). Training options appear limited to CSCS cards (construction health and safety certificates) and SIA badges (security licences). This might be helpful for some, but this is not reflective of the varied skills needs of the economy: "I've worked mainly in offices all my life. Believe it or not they sent me on a course for construction [laughs] . . . I was given the choice of doing the SIA card or the CSCS card, and it was with the implied threat that if you don't do one of these courses we'll sanction you" (male, 59, Universal Credit claimant, cited in Jones 2019).

The support available also appears to be highly variable, with no minimum service agreements, there is a reliance on individual work coaches to connect jobseekers to suitable skills training. Training is slightly more developed for young jobseekers. Sector-based work academies, for example, provide pre-employment training, work experience placements and a guaranteed job interview, and have been found to have a positive impact on employment outcomes (DWP 2016). While in April 2021, as part of its Train and Progress (TaP) initiative, the government increased the number of weeks Universal Credit claimants can study on a full-time basis from 8 weeks up to 12 weeks, this is unfortunately only a temporary measure, which at the time of writing, was due to come to an end in April 2023 (Gable 2021).

Overall, the available statistics show that the benefits system is failing to provide a pathway into training: according to the latest statistical release on Further Education for Benefit Claimants, the proportion of benefit spells including training has plateaued at just over 6 per cent (DfE/DWP 2019) (see Figure 8.1)

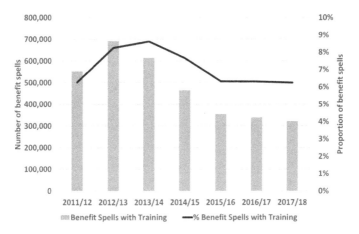

Figure 8.1   Volume and proportion of benefit spells with training,
2011/12–2017/18

Source: DfE/DWP (2019) Further Education for Benefit Claimants
Experimental Statistics.

The welfare system is also not functioning well as a route
into apprenticeships – the government's flagship skills policy. In
2017/18, only 6 per cent of apprenticeship starts were by apprentices on benefits in the 6 months before starting, down from 14
per cent in 2013/14 (see Figure 8.2).

Not only is our welfare system bad at linking people to these
training opportunities – it is getting worse. Why is this the case,
given that our welfare and apprenticeship systems (and skills system more generally) essentially share the same aim of facilitating
work entry and progression?

The answer is that this is another casualty of the UK's work
first approach. Whereas training and education is a key aspect of
employment support in many other countries, it is sidelined in the
UK. From time-to-time small-scale pilots have hinted at potential shifts towards more progressive human capital development

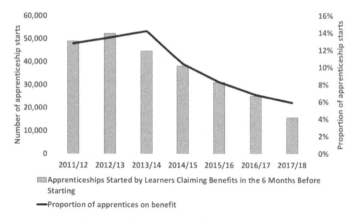

Figure 8.2 Volume and proportion of apprenticeship starts where learners were on benefits six months before starting, 2011/12–2017/18

Source: DfE/DWP (2019) Further Education for Benefit Claimants Experimental Statistics.

approaches in UK active labour market policies (see Lindsay *et al.* 2007 on employability pilots). These, however, have never become part of the mainstream offer of our public employment service. Claimants must not be "idle", but also apparently not engage in such activities as might improve their prospects in the labour market. Under the work first model, time spent learning and developing new skills is time not spent applying for and being available for work.

This is short-sighted. Human capital development approaches, which invest in training and skills for jobseekers have better long-term employment outcomes (Card *et al.* 2015; Osikominu 2021) (see Box 8.1 for an example). They have also been found to have larger mental health benefits (Wang *et al.* 2020). For those moving into new sectors, retraining takes time, but arguably time well spent as the workforce needs to reskill in order to support development in new areas of growth including green and digital technologies.

Not only does the UK welfare system appear not to be supporting claimants into training, it can also create additional barriers to engage. In some instances, access to the small amount of skills and training provision on offer is conditional on people making a claim. In order to access training through a sector-based work academy, for example, young people need to be making a claim for unemployment benefit and be referred by their work coach. This immediately excludes the 50 per cent of young people who are not in employment, education or training who, despite being eligible, forgo their right to claim (Jones *et al.* 2018). There are two issues to address here: first, ensuring that the benefits system opens up pathways into training, but does not exclude those eligible for but reluctant to claim; second, making a serious attempt to tackle non-take up.

SKILLS SUPPORT NOT MANDATED LEARNING

In saying that the welfare system should create opportunities for people to participate in education and training, we do not advocate strong-arming the unemployed and low paid into training courses. In the same way that people need to be given more choice about the jobs that they apply for and move into, people need to be offered quality training options – good enough that they want, and see the value of, engaging in.

In our current system, where an individual's unemployment is attributed, at least in part, to a lack of skills, they can be mandated by the benefit system to enrol on and participate in courses to improve their skills, or risk losing their unemployment benefit. So-called "skills conditionality" has been justified by policymakers who point to both the benefits of participating in learning, but also low levels of take-up of skills interventions amongst the unemployed, and high levels of drop-out following

Jobcentre referrals to voluntary provision (DWP/BIS 2010, 2011). Mandated training is justified on paternalistic grounds – it's for their own good. As we can see from the participation statistics above, this doesn't appear to be happening very much, but it is nevertheless the wrong approach, and expanding the skills offer for claimants should not be done in this way.

The evidence base on skills conditionality and education and training provision within active labour market policy more widely is limited (most analyses don't separate out the various conditional activities). However, such an approach runs contrary to what a long history of research on adult education on the reasons behind adults' (non-)participation in education tells us (see Boeren 2016 for a helpful overview). At an individual level, whether or not an adult chooses to participate in available learning opportunities depends on whether or not they are motivated, confident and able to do so. As Knud Illeris, Danish professor of lifelong learning, explains: "adults are not very inclined to learn something they are not interested in, or in which they cannot see the meaning or importance" (2006: 17).

Mandated learning for unmotivated adults will therefore be of little benefit. Skills conditionality might make more people *attend* training, however it is unlikely to help adults to improve their skills, and may even have a negative impact on their desire to engage in learning in the future. In 2006, O'Grady and Atkin carried out a study exploring the experiences of jobseekers mandated to attend Skills for Life (literacy and numeracy) training in the mid-2000s. They found that, although people attended classes, participants were typically unmotivated, failing to explain why they were attending the training, any learning aims or the value of improving their skills. Comparing voluntary and mandated learners, the latter were found to be much more likely to be "passive recipients" or reject training completely.

More recently, Rolfe (2012), in her DWP-commissioned evaluation of skills conditionality found that participants "accepted training offers more from resignation than active interest" – a finding reiterated by frontline Jobcentre staff: "Mandating makes them turn up but not necessarily take part in training". This study also found that Jobcentre staff can frustrate attempts to participate in learning: "some jobseekers who had organized training themselves found their arrangements disrupted by the requirement to attend training through the pilot". Requiring someone to participate in a training course, under threat of financial sanction positions education as a negative punishment rather than a positive opportunity. It is not the way to engender enthusiasm for lifelong learning.

Wanting to engage in learning activities and improve skills requires an individual to identify their skills "need", to recognize the value in addressing it and believe that they are capable of doing so. The opportunities also have to be there. For many adults – contrary to demonizing narratives – accessing or progressing in employment is a key motivation for engaging in training and education (Aldridge & Hughes 2012). Courses with an occupational focus have been found to have more positive responses (Rolfe 2012).

This is the case even for those with significant barriers to labour market participation. In one study of homeless service users, for example, employment-related benefits such as gaining qualifications, increasing their employability, and getting a job were seen as important motivators for engaging in learning and skills provision (Luby & Welch 2006).

Barriers to learning participation are complex, and a combination of practical and situational barriers, often combined with low confidence and self-esteem can make adults reluctant or unable to engage (Jones 2021b). For some, poor performance at school and fears about assessment and testing, reinforced by "repeated exposure to failure", deter many from engaging with learning in adulthood (Olisa *et al.* 2010).

WHAT NEEDS TO CHANGE?

The role of our welfare system in encouraging and facilitating learning participation needs urgent attention. The enduring chasm between the UK's welfare and skills system must be addressed. Although both systems share common objectives in relation to equipping people with the skills and capabilities they need to succeed in the labour market and access economic opportunities, they are frustratingly separate in design and delivery. The onus is on "empowered" work coaches to connect jobseekers to relevant training opportunities and there is very little visibility/transparency about the extent to which Jobcentres are effectively supporting participation in lifelong learning.

But how empowered can they be when their objectives are firmly centred on moving people into work quickly? Jobcentre staff have highlighted a lack of occupational courses in some local areas (Rolfe 2012), and the difficulty of understanding a complex patchwork of skills provision offered by different training providers, local colleges and community organizations, that differs both in different devolved nations and at a subnational level across different local authorities (Heins & Bennett 2018).

Importantly, given the potential for synergies, overlaps, and even potential conflicts, between the DWP's priorities, and those of the Department for Business, Energy and Industrial Strategy (BEIS) and the Department for Education, the DWP and these departments should develop a cross-departmental strategy on lifelong learning. Together they should be creating a learner-focused system which is informed, not dictated, by employers in core growth sectors. As part of this, there should be an emphasis on supporting people to develop core literacy, numeracy and digital skills and also the skills needed for accessing good quality jobs in key growth sectors.

An inquiry into the learning aspirations and barriers to learning for those who are unemployed or in low-paid work should be a priority as new skills investments are made. Skills policy should always explicitly consider and demonstrate how it will support people who are unemployed or on a low income, and ensure that the benefit system provides a helpful pathway into these opportunities, rather than a barrier.

BOX 8.1 CASE STUDY: WORKADVANCE, UNITED STATES

WorkAdvance in the United States has been identified as a promising example of sector-based initiatives designed to support work entry and progression (see Sissons 2020; Green 2021). Through providing people with employment-related skills in high-demand sectors, it aimed to support people on a low income to progress in the labour market. The Work-Advance model involves matching individuals to suitable opportunities, providing sector-related pre-employment support including career advancement coaching, and sector-specific training leading to qualifications and skills that are valued by employers.

Working closely with employers, the programme supports people into jobs that offer genuine opportunities for development and progression and participants continue to be supported while in work through coaching and training support. The programme aims to meet the needs of participants by supporting them into quality job opportunities at the same time as meeting employer needs through recruitment and addressing skills shortages (Sissons 2020). An evaluation of WorkAdvance showed it to have positive impacts on employment and earnings, including amongst participants who were long-term unemployed (Hendra *et al.* 2016).

It is striking that recent announcements and policy developments in relation to skills do not mention how new policies and investments will work practically for those who are unemployed or on a low income. There was only one mention of Jobcentres in the latest Skills For Jobs white paper (DfE 2021). Government also needs to ensure that those seeking to access further education opportunities are better supported. Currently, higher education students can access maintenance loans, making it possible to reduce the amount they work and participate in study, whereas further education students cannot access such maintenance support, cutting off this option for many (Henehan 2021).

We need a learning and skills revolution, which inspires rather than mandates. It should help people navigate what can often be a confusing array of options, advising about the job opportunities available in a changing labour market and how engaging in training and skills support can help them to access those opportunities.

9

Social infrastructure

"I'd have to have like breakfast clubs, after-school clubs and the 3-year-old only gets three hours a day paid nursery so I'd have to top that up. So, with that and petrol and parking, it just wouldn't be worth it."

Young woman, Sheffield
(cited in Kumar *et al.* 2014)

So far, we have focused on how state policies aimed at low-paid workers – on welfare and skills – have the effect of undermining bargaining power in the workplace. However, the state's effects on low-paid workers have much broader scope. In the final chapters of this book we turn our attention to wider factors that influence the labour market, exploring the role of social infrastructure and state regulation in supporting good work and overcoming labour market exclusion.

Starting with the former, we show how degradation of social infrastructure – from declining local bus services to childcare services that don't meet the shift patterns of low-paid workers – conspire to create barriers to work, especially for women. As we show, childcare and transport are not only social policy issues but fundamental to tackling low-pay low-productivity Britain.

CHILDCARE

Self-evidently, childcare is essential to parents being able to work: no parent can go out to work unless someone is looking after their children. The responsibility normally falls on mothers: employment rates in mixed-sex couples with children under 12 are 20 percentage points lower for women than for men; average hours of work are more than 40 per cent lower; nine out of ten lone parents are women. Time-use data shows that women spend twice as much time as fathers looking after children (Wishart *et al.* 2019). Seven out of ten mothers of children aged below four say that having reliable childcare helps them to go out to work (DfE 2019).

Childcare in the UK is more expensive than most other high-income countries. Support for childcare is a mix of free and subsidized provision, support through the welfare system, and tax reliefs on childcare expenditure. Taking these into account, the net expenditure on childcare for couples with two children aged two and three using formal childcare is likely to be around one third of the average wage. For lone parents, net expenditure is lower. However, at 10 per cent of the average wage, there are still only four countries in the OECD with higher rates (see Figure 9.1).

Furthermore, the cost of childcare has been rising faster than either prices or average earnings. Between 2008 and 2021, full-time nursery costs for a child under two in England rose by 69 per cent (Daycare Trust 2008; Jarvie *et al.* 2021) whereas inflation and average earnings rose by 30 per cent and 29 per cent over the same period. The net cost borne by families has reduced for better-off parents in recent years – probably due to the Tax-Free Childcare scheme – but, for the lowest earners has increased significantly (see Figure 9.2).

There is a system of subsidy available through the benefit system for childcare costs. Eighty-five per cent of costs of up to £175 per week for a first child and £300 for multiple children can be included in a claimant's maximum amount. Payments are

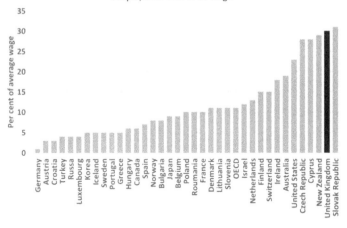

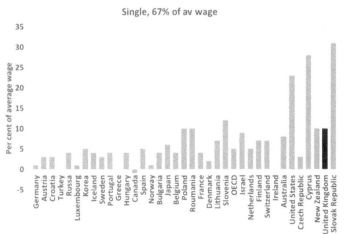

Figure 9.1 Net childcare costs as a percentage of the average wage for different types of families, each with two children aged two and three

Source: OECD.

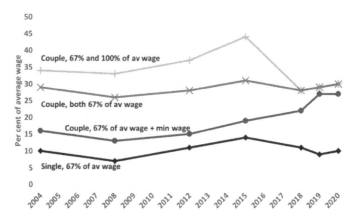

Figure 9.2   Net childcare costs for UK families with two children aged two and three

Source: OECD.

then reduced as incomes rise. However, it is a common complaint that childcare costs have to be paid up front and the subsidy is only paid in arrears. The effect is that low-income families without savings struggle to meet these costs as this quote from recent research by the Learning and Work Institute and Gingerbread demonstrates:

> [Y]ou have to pay first and then you claim it back. I managed to borrow some money from a friend to be able to do that ... it was quite difficult and it's awkward ... I understand why people don't go back to work because by the time you sort out childcare ... I was paying £30 a day. Then you think, I have only earned £50 today. You do get it back, but it can be up to 4–6 weeks before you get that money back and they stretch that over the year. (Grace; cited in Dromey *et al.* 2020)

Furthermore, a critical issue with formal childcare is its inflexibility. Working patterns for low-paid workers in industries such as care, hospitality and retail typically revolve around shifts. The 30 hours of free childcare offered to three- and four-year-olds with working parents is usually structured to align with the school day and does not operate in school holidays. For older children, after-school clubs and breakfast clubs – so-called "wraparound" childcare – effectively extends the school day for working parents – often providing care between 8am and 6pm. However, for pre-school children, formal provision to cater for these hours is often very expensive (Jarvie *et al*. 2021). Whilst 8am to 6pm weekday childcare might be sufficient for workers with regular office hours, it does not reflect the reality of shift patterns in retail, hospitality and care where earlier or much later hours of work are common, including at weekends. As mentioned above, holiday childcare is a critical issue for many parents. School holidays amount to at least 13 weeks each year, and more affordable formal childcare options often don't cover the holidays.

The consequence of the high cost and inflexibility of formal childcare is that the reality for many working families is that they have to rely on a mix of formal and family childcare. In 2017, Age UK reported that two-fifths of the UK's grandparents have provided regular childcare for their grandchildren. Moreover, nearly half of mothers in paid work in England with a child under five say that having relatives help with childcare helps them to go out to work (DfE 2019). The same survey also records 17 per cent of mothers having access to some free/cheap childcare, 13 per cent of mothers in couples arranging work at times when their partner is not working, and 7 per cent getting help from friends.

This is a story that is well-told. The annual Coram Childcare Survey (Jarvie *et al*. 2021) and Department for Education Childcare and Early Years Survey (DfE 2019) document thoroughly the costs and juggling required of working parents. However, what is less well-documented is the effect that childcare has on progression in the labour market. As we have seen, managing childcare is a juggling act involving various combinations of formal childcare, grandparents, organizing shifts to fit around partners' working hours. Apart from being stressful, the negotiation of these complex arrangements takes time and, as there are dependencies between them, if one piece of the jigsaw is put in jeopardy, the whole picture is at risk.

In terms of career progression, the consequences of this complexity are twofold. It is vital to have work that can be managed alongside available and affordable childcare options. Not only must shifts fit around planned hours, but there has to be some resilience – i.e. flexibility – from employers to be able to manage the inevitable calls from the school or childcare provider that a child is ill and needs collecting immediately. This requirement for work that fits around childcare limits the pool of potential employers. The consequence is that employers know they face less competition from other employers for their staff and can hold down wages compared to more competitive labour markets.

Furthermore, we know that job mobility – being able to change jobs and employers – is important for pay growth. For example, in 2018, the ONS reported that median hourly earnings growth for "job changers" was 7.3 per cent compared to 3.0 per cent for "job stayers" (ONS 2019). Having childcare-related limits on the number of potential employers reduces the prospects for job mobility: if fewer jobs or employers offer the right package of hours and flexibility to make possible the childcare juggle, then there are fewer opportunities for the pay growth that comes with being able to change jobs. Crucially, it also increases the risk of jeopardizing the hard-won settlement that is the parent's current childcare arrangements. If negotiations have taken place with employers, grandparents, partners and others to reach a working childcare arrangement, a move to a new job that throws these arrangements up in the air can feel like a significant risk.

TRANSPORT

The point about the above discussion is that the need to juggle complex childcare arrangements becomes a constraint on labour supply: available hours are constrained by the childcare options available, and the pool of potential employers is smaller than otherwise. The consequence is similar to the economic theory of the one-employer town: the power of workers is reduced and the (monopsony) power of the employer increases, holding down wages and reducing the prospects for wage growth. However, childcare is not the only public service that has a material impact on these issues.

Public transport is regarded by policymakers as an essential part of the infrastructure for a successful economy. What this means for people on lower incomes is good bus services. Whilst households in the top two-fifths of the income distribution take more trips each year by train than by bus, households with the lowest fifth of incomes take three times as many trips by bus as by train (DfT 2021d). However, outside of London, local services are often poor, as evidenced by the total number of bus journeys falling for decades (Figure 9.3).

In response, many of the City Deals negotiated between cities in England and central government include the power for the city region to regulate bus services (e.g. Ames 2020) – a reversal of more than 30 years of policy. There are specific ways in which bus service problems affect low-paid workers in particular. Services after 6pm are particularly poor, which causes problems for people with shift patterns in sectors such as retail, care and hospitality where very few jobs are 9 to 5 (DfT 2021a). Typically, patterns of bus routes in and around cities are radial – running into and out of the city centre. However, such routes are often useless for care workers moving around suburbs and crossing fare boundaries. Fares are also expensive. Since 1995, in cities outside London, fares have nearly doubled in real terms (DfT 2021b). Given that

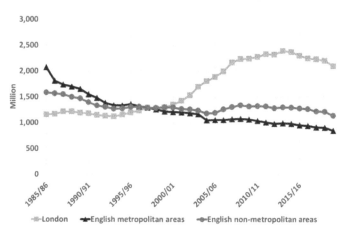

Figure 9.3   Bus journeys in England, 1985/86–2019/20

Source: Department for Transport, bus statistics (DfT 2021c).

bus companies are in the private sector, it is unsurprising that they might wish to concentrate services on times of the day and routes that are most profitable.

The fact that public transport outside London is poor should come as no surprise. IPPR North has documented for some years disparities in transport expenditure between London and the rest of England (Raikes 2019). The question is what effect this has on low-paid workers.

It is hard to test the counterfactual – what would have happened had public transport been better. However, the Institute of Transport Studies has found that 77 per cent of jobseekers whom they interviewed did not have regular access to a car. This study also found that 20 per cent of jobseekers in their sample had either not applied for a job or attended an interview, turned down a job, or left a job due to a lack of a suitable or affordable bus services (Johnson & Mackie 2013).

The Social Exclusion Unit reported two decades ago that mismatches between the location and hours of work of job vacancies and local bus services was a barrier to employment (Social Exclusion Unit 2003). In 2010, research by the National Foundation for Educational Research found that 20 per cent of young people who want to participate in education cite transport costs as a major barrier (Spielhofer *et al.* 2008). In 2018, the Southern Policy Centre carried out a study that demonstrated the particular salience of transport issues for work outcomes for people living in rural areas (Boswell *et al.* 2018).

It is also clear that the issues of transport and caring commitments interact for low-paid workers. Caring responsibilities usually come with binding constraints on a person's time: there is usually no flexibility to be late for the school gate, the after-school club, or to pick up from a childminder. In 2016, a survey of 1,000 low-paid workers in retail found that having a job close to home was the top reason given for working in retail (Ussher 2016).

In 2018, the Institute for Fiscal Studies found evidence of a relationship between transport and the motherhood pay penalty, with the gap in commuting time between men and women increasing significantly after the birth of the first child (Joyce & Keiller 2018). If there is no flexibility on pick-up time, then having reliable transport to reach the school gate, after-school club, or childminder is essential. The absence of reliable transport will again reduce the pool of jobs that workers in this position can consider.

Caring responsibilities and poor transport services therefore combine to limit severely the potential pool of jobs that many women can consider, once again reducing the possibilities for progression and reducing workers' power in the labour market. This chapter demonstrates that investing in transport and quality care services must become a part of mainstream economic policy-making if they are to support rather than constrain low-paid women seeking to improve their employment opportunities.

10

State regulation

"The trouble with government regulation of the market is that it prohibits capitalist acts between consenting adults".

Robert Nozick (1978)

"Regulations level the playing field for everyone competing for our business. Because of regulations, good companies that do right by their customers don't have to compete against cheaters.... That's good for customers and good for upstart competitors who think they have a better product to offer."

Senator Elizabeth Warren (2018)

This final chapter considers regulation of the labour market. The starting point for such discussions is usually that there is a trade-off between protecting workers and strengthening the economy, and the political process decides where on the spectrum policy will end up. We show that in fact a reluctance to protect working conditions exacerbates the imbalance of power between workers and employers and contributes to the low-pay low-productivity equilibrium that locks too many people into low-paid work, and slows down the UK's economic performance.

CONTESTED POLICY

Labour market regulation has been a contested area of economic policy for centuries. When the first Factory Acts started limiting children's hours of work, there were voices that protested at the economic damage such restrictions would cause. Lord Lauderdale said in the House of Lords that he opposed the Cotton Mills and Factory Act of 1819 because it violated "the great principle of Political Economy that labour ought to be free" (Walker 1941). This Act prohibited employing children under the age of nine in the cotton industry and limited work for those aged nine to 16 to 12 hours a day (UK Parliament, n.d.). Over the course of the nineteenth century, legislation limited further children's and later women's hours of work, introduced factory inspectors and the first new rules for managing dangerous machinery (Bloy, n.d.).

Today, we take for granted a much wider range of protections. The Contracts of Employment Act 1963 brought with it a right to a written specification of hours of work, pay rates and notice periods. The 1960s and 1970s saw the first protections against discrimination at work, covering race and sex. Recent years have seen these protections extended to cover disability, sexual orientation, age, religion and belief. For two decades, there has been a national minimum wage, limits on hours of work for all workers – not just those in factories – and rights to a minimum amount of paid holiday leave each year.

Just as with the first Factory Acts, each of these pieces of legislation has been contested. In a House of Commons debate in 1998 on the new limits on working hours and rights to paid holiday, John Redwood MP, Shadow Secretary of State for Trade and Industry, said:

Eighteen months on, there is growing evidence of a downturn made in Downing Street, with closure after closure, job loss after job loss and problem after problem. The

Minister must answer on that general issue as it applies to this debate. Will not he concede that every such regulation, reducing flexibility and imposing additional costs, makes it more difficult for the enterprise economy to work and for us to achieve the improvement in living standards and in terms and conditions that always comes when an economy is growing or flourishing?

The paradox may be that, through the regulations, more people will lose their jobs and fewer will have decent living standards and quality of employment, because the regulations are part of the process by which the golden economic legacy is being squandered. (Hansard, HC Deb. 27 October 1998)

EQUITY–EFFICIENCY TRADE-OFF

The question of whether labour market regulation is justified is normally presented as a trade-off: on the one hand, rules can offer important protections for working people; on the other, the very same rules may slow down the economy. When the question is put like this, the answer is to be found in the respective value placed upon better living conditions for working people versus the desire to grow the economy and create jobs. Some will incline towards the former and others the latter.

What unifies the two sides is that there is a trade-off to be had between protecting workers and maximizing economic output – you can't have both and must choose which is valued more. Economists call this an equity–efficiency trade-off: do we prefer the greater equity from rules that protect workers or the efficiency that comes from stronger economic growth? Once this trade-off is accepted, the job of the political process is to decide whether and how much we prefer the "equity" that arises from employment protection or the "efficiency" that comes from higher output.

One point made by those on the "efficiency" side of this debate is that those who favour the "equity" of higher labour standards are simply protecting current workers at the expense of those out of work. The argument is that labour market regulation increases the costs of hiring people. This might not matter to those already in work but reduces the extent to which employers might expand their workforce if demand allows. Thus higher levels of regulation is likely to suppress employment and benefit those already in work – insiders – at the expense of those looking for work – outsiders. The point of this argument is that it adds to the case against labour market regulation.

So, does this efficiency–equity trade-off hold: do we have to make a choice between protecting workers through better working conditions and higher economic growth? The arguments against this framework have a number of elements. Better conditions for workers can translate into higher satisfaction at work, which results in higher performance and lower staff turnover. Lower staff turnover in turn means that employers get longer to reap the benefits of investing in training and developing the skills of their staff so more training happens. This in turn leads to higher productivity and increased firm performance.

So much for the theoretical arguments – what does the evidence say? One obvious example of an area where there has been lots of policy activity is the minimum wage. Over the past two decades, a number of countries and states/regions within countries have introduced minimum wages, and gone on to raise them significantly. Did these measures cost jobs? In March 2019, the UK government commissioned Arin Dube to review the evidence on exactly this question (Hansard HC Deb. 13 March 2019). As shown in Chapter 2 on productivity, there is strong evidence that this has not cost jobs in the way feared in the traditional "equity vs efficiency" account of labour market regulation (Dube 2019).

In 1998, the UK government's introduction of the Working Time Directive introduced a maximum 48 hours working week and a right to four weeks of paid holiday for employees. In 2008, holiday entitlements were increased to 28 days a year (four weeks plus eight days of public holidays). Once again, the "equity vs efficiency" framework would suggest that this policy should have had an economic cost. However, an evaluation of the policy's impact on the labour market published by the Department for Business Innovation & Skills failed to find any such impact (BIS 2014).

Improving standards of safety at work is one of the major success stories of policy over the past century. In 1900, 4,400 people died in Britain as a result of a workplace injury. In the years after the Second World War, the figure stood at around 2,000. In the latest year of data, there were 88 such fatalities (Health and Safety Executive 2021).[1]

Although health and safety legislation is criticized by some as being a burdensome, pointless, cost on society, the cost to a business of a worker accident is far higher and, crucially, less predictable. Furthermore, the costs are not just borne by the business and (obviously) by the individual worker but also by the state. For example, in 2018/19, an estimated 16,400 people withdrew permanently from the labour market as a result of a workplace injury or work-related ill health (HSE 2020). Each such withdrawal generates higher healthcare costs, reduces tax income and creates higher benefits payments. Overall, the estimated total cost to the UK of workplace injury and work-related ill health was £16.2

---

1 Throughout the period to 1980, there were many changes in legislation that increased the scope of requirements to report fatal injuries to the authorities, and changes in enforcement. There have also been changes in the numbers of people employed in the industries covered by the legislation in force at the time. So the figures are not comparable from year-to-year. However, they give a broad picture of how deaths at work have reduced substantially over the past century.

billion in 2018/19. However, this was split into £9.6 billion born by workers, £3.2 billion by employers, and £3.5 billion by government (HSE 2020).

The Arin Dube review found that one of the ways in which employers respond to higher minimum wages is to look for improvements in productivity to be able to afford to pay higher wages (Dube 2019: 52–3). Similarly, the evidence from the Health and Safety Executive is that the costs of workplace accidents are so substantial that regulation in this area saves rather than costs. The point to draw is that in both of these cases an equity vs efficiency trade-off does not exist. The action that might be thought of in the equity camp – higher minimum wages and strong safety rules – actually increases efficiency. In the case of the Working Time Directive, there was no evidence of a trade-off existing.

Given that there is evidence that there is not a trade-off between doing good through labour market regulation and improving productivity or achieving high levels of economic growth, we need to dispense with the baseline assumption that all regulation of the labour market is burdensome.

This raises the question of the arguments in favour of labour market regulation. Here, the balance of costs of workplace accidents reveals an important point. Clearly the majority of the responsibility to reduce workplace accidents lies with employers. Yet, according to the Health and Safety Executive, they bear only a fifth of the costs when they fail to do so. This is a classic case of what economists call an externality where the decision-maker doesn't bear all of the costs of their actions. What is inevitable is that, if employers only factor in their own costs into their decision-making, they will underprovide safety measures and leave workers and the state to pick up the majority of the resulting bill. The answer to this externality problem is for the state to require from employers obligations equivalent to the costs that their actions might impose on employees and the state.

Of course, many employers rightly feel a duty of care to their staff and take seriously not relying on the state to pick up the costs of their own failures. But it only takes a small number of employers not to take this view for others to feel undercut by competition from their less scrupulous neighbours. Ensuring a level playing field for fair competition is another important justification for state regulation.

This discussion reveals two important reasons for state regulation. Firstly, where externalities occur – costs borne by someone other than the employer – it is likely that at least some employers will not voluntarily provide the right standards. Secondly, relying on voluntary compliance with standards leaves good employers at risk of being undercut by competition from those who are not.

What the Arin Dube evidence on the minimum wage shows is that regulation can be productivity enhancing. It is not difficult to conceptualize why this might be so. When employers invest in training and developing the skills of their staff, not only does it benefit the company in question but the members of staff and society as a whole benefit too. In economists' jargon, this is a positive externality – benefits that don't go to the person bearing the costs. As before, if the employer makes their decision based only on their own costs, then the amount of training provided by employers will be less than society would ideally like.

State intervention to deal with this positive externality could take the form of subsidies to employers to provide training or it could take the form of compulsion to provide a certain amount of training. The former would effectively mean the state paying for its share of the benefits. As employers wouldn't have to meet the entirety of costs, the amount of provision would increase towards the level that society might desire. The latter approach would mean requiring employers to meet the state's bill when they might not otherwise choose to do so.

As shown in the discussion on the minimum wage, labour

market regulation can incentivize employers to look for productivity improvements. There may also be overlaps – complementarities – between the skills required to meet regulations and those needed for higher levels of management skills. However, these benefits will not be the same for all forms of regulation – they will vary depending on the regulation in question, and on how the rules are framed and enforced. While evidence does exist on minimum wages, it is relatively thin in other areas of regulation. More research in this area is clearly needed.

But if labour standards really do produce such benefits, why then do businesses not all take the "high road" and improve labour standards? Firstly, some of the benefits are public goods – i.e. benefits to society as a whole, rather than to the individual firm. The obvious example is training, where for virtually any transferable skills, it is in principle impossible for a firm to capture all of the return on the investment in training because of the risk of staff leaving for another employer. In that situation, firms will *always* underprice the true value of higher levels of skills, and there is therefore a role for the state. This applies *whenever* there is a positive externality – a gain from higher labour standards that is not felt just by the employer but by society as a whole.

The second reason is information: where employers are unable to calculate accurately the return on taking the "high road" and improving labour standards. Productivity is an obvious example of this, where many small businesses lack knowledge of their own productivity, and lack knowledge of what improves it. Many small businesses are operating on the basis of manager instinct and rules of thumb (Green *et al*. 2018). In this context, personal histories of managers become an important source of their information base. If, historically, the UK has underperformed in management, the necessity of improving in this regard is less clear to the small business owner-manager.

The third is competition. In theory, the long-term returns to higher labour standards should lead to companies holding their nerve, and holding out for the higher returns. However, in many markets the competitive environment means that it is difficult for managers not to answer quickly the risk of being undercut by lower quality competitors.

For a number of years, major business organizations such as the Confederation of British Industry, have been advocating that the UK should not lower its regulatory standards as it leaves the European Union (CBI 2018). Their argument is that businesses need a stable regulatory environment where they cannot be unfairly undercut, but that the preference of the businesses that they represent is for that level to represent a high standard.

The implication is that there is supressed demand from businesses for higher standards, but individual businesses cannot take the risk of being a radical first mover in this area – they need the protection of fitting in with universal standards to avoid the risk of being undercut.

For all three of these reasons, there is an economic justification for state intervention to improve labour standards. Intervention may take the form of subsidies to account for positive externalities (such as higher levels of skills in the economy) so that businesses take decisions that are better for society as a whole. Or they may take the form of rules that set minimum standards so that businesses that want to improve labour standards are not undercut by others.

However, while the theory is clear – that there are economic reasons why state intervention is necessary to ensure labour standards and high quality work – this does not answer the question of the level at which such subsidies or regulations should be set. To return to the theory, if a subsidy for a training course were set at a level above the benefit received by society, the course would appear too cheap to employers and they would "over-consume" the course compared to the ideal level that society needs. Similarly, if new rules were legislated to require all employees to be provided with their hours of work in a contract of employment,[2] would this be too onerous for employers (and therefore reduce employment) or would knowing working hours in advance improve the lives of low-paid workers and, potentially, improve the quality of management, employee engagement and productivity in many firms?

The answer to this conundrum is that it depends: on the value to society produced by the training course, and on the benefits of knowing working hours in advance. Each potential regulation raises its own questions. In the case of minimum wages, the fact that there have been different rates set in lots of jurisdictions provide natural experiments that allow experts such as Arin Dube, quoted above, to analyse their effect. However, in many aspects of regulation, the evidence does not exist to a sufficient degree.

The response to this is frequently to retreat to rules of thumb unconstrained by evidence: that there must be an equity vs efficiency trade-off, or that lower rules and regulations are always good for productivity. However, what we have seen in respect of those labour standards where the data does exist is that the question is far more open. Minimum wages do not, generally, reduce employment, and therefore are highly likely to enhance productivity to some degree. Working time rules don't cost jobs and might enhance productivity. So, the evidence on this question is not definitive, but it certainly does not sit on the efficiency-over-equity side of the debate.

The final consideration is to reflect on the UK labour market over the past two decades. The highest employment rates ever seen have not delivered prosperity or good working conditions for large numbers of low-paid workers. Working to a default assumption that there is always a trade-off between equity and efficiency has not delivered the productivity improvements we might have

---

2 The Contracts of Employment Acts of 1963 and 1972 sought to put in place precisely this protection but the rise in zero-hours contracts demonstrates that this protection was not watertight.

hoped for – in fact the opposite. Given that the labour market outcomes give no support at all to the traditional view that lower regulation means higher growth, and the evidence that we do have in relation to some forms of regulation suggests that the opposite might be true, it is time to question our prior assumptions about labour market regulation.

This means two things. Equity vs efficiency trade-offs have proved a poor guide to the labour market of the past two decades so we should not assume that we must always choose one or the other. Whether a piece of regulation harms the labour market or helps it is a question we should test with an open mind as there is a decent chance that higher levels of regulation might well be part of the story of moving us towards a higher pay higher productivity economy.

ENFORCEMENT

The discussion in this chapter has focused on what our rules should be, and whether there is a trade-off between economic efficiency and protecting workers. But rights are not worth the paper they are written on if they are not enforced and the reality is that there is widespread non-compliance. The Low Pay Commission estimates that 440,000 workers were paid less than the minimum wage in April 2019 (Low Pay Commission 2021) and the problem has been getting worse in recent years (Judge & Stansbury 2020).

Analysis by the Resolution Foundation also finds that one in 20 workers say they do not receive paid holiday (a right from day one in any job) and roughly one in ten workers report not receiving a payslip (a mandatory requirement) (Cominetti & Judge 2019). These violations tend to be clustered in more precarious forms of work – including zero-hours and temporary contracts. It is likely that statistics will underestimate the true scale of rights violations if, for example, workers are understandably scared to report.

Multiple state bodies are responsible for enforcement in the UK. Her Majesty's Revenue and Customs (HMRC) is responsible for investigating minimum wage compliance, the Employment Agencies Standards Inspectorate has oversight of employment agencies and the Gangmaster and Labour Abuse Authority has a brief to protect vulnerable and exploited workers. However, as the Resolution Foundation point out, their resources are dwarfed by the scale of the challenges they are tasked with addressing.

Instead, there is a reliance on individuals to assert their rights where there are breaches. But it is workers who are most vulnerable to labour market violations that are the least likely to make an application to an employment tribunal. Whilst those in atypical forms of work and those working in elementary occupations are most likely to be exposed to violations, they are less likely than other groups – such as managers and directors – to take action against their employer (Cominetti & Judge 2019).

In a recent study, Rose *et al.* (2017) identified a range of reasons why claims are not pursued, including the difficulty in proving a claim, being unable to afford the costs of a claim, wanting to keep their job despite the dispute with the employer, needing a reference to get another job, and dealing with the birth of a child at the time of trying to pursue pregnancy-related discrimination. They give an example of Kim, working in the care sector on a zero-hours contract typically working 40 hours a week who asked for adjustments due to her pregnancy, but who had her hours reduced to eight. She submitted a grievance to her employer, but they took two months to send her a rejection of her case that coincided with the birth of her baby, giving her only five days to respond. She abandoned the claim: "If I'd looked into it or had time to talk to Citizens Advice, I probably did have the right to ask for longer maybe even just on grounds of having a baby ... but at that time ... I felt really deflated by it and that was draining in itself so I didn't even think like I should go and ask somebody what my rights are" (Rose *et al.* 2017).

The Low Pay Commission and others have stressed the need for a strong strategic direction on enforcement (Low Pay Commission 2021). As part of its Good Work Plan, the government has recently consulted on bringing its various agencies together into a new single enforcement body for employment rights (BEIS 2021). Other changes included in a proposed Employment Bill include improved redundancy rights for people on maternity leave, paid neonatal leave, a right to request a more predictable and stable contract, and a requirement for hospitality businesses to pass on all tips. However, at the time of writing there is growing concern that this commitment to good work is falling off the agenda. The post of Director of Labour Market Enforcement remained vacant for ten months (Institute of Employment Rights 2021) and there is no timetable for this Employment Bill to be brought forward to Parliament (Taylor 2021).

When the state's infrastructure for ensuring that all employers keep to minimum standards is weak, the effects are felt not just on the workers in these firms, but from the competitive pressure from those who skirt or evade the rules. Robust competition is a necessary condition of a productive economy, and the failure to enforce existing rules undermines the fairness of the competitive environment, reducing standards for all.

Conclusion

What needs to change?

When Beveridge was writing about the Giant of "Idleness" in 1942, his concern was primarily about the unemployment that had scarred the economy for two decades prior to the Second World War. Eighty years on, this is no longer the pressing issue. Today, we have historically high rates of employment, but also our highest ever rates of in-work poverty. The UK is stuck in a low-pay, low-productivity rut. We have a two-tier economy in which far too many people are working in poor quality jobs, with barely any training and little chance of getting on. Growth in the gig economy and short-hours work has brought insecurity to the labour market in defiance of employment protections built up steadily since the Second World War.

Our economic and policy debate has failed to keep up with the reality of today's economy. Today, too often Conservative government ministers trumpet high employment rates whilst many in the Labour Party talk about the need to create jobs. The conversation feels like it is stuck in the 1980s or early 1990s and misses the elephant in the room: too many of those jobs don't enable people to enjoy a decent standard of living and nor do they provide the security, dignity and prospects for progression to which we should all have access. Today's problem with the labour market is not a shortage of work but a shortage of *good quality* work: inclusive, decently-paid, and secure, with prospects for advancement. If Beveridge were surveying the labour market today, instead of the unemployment of the 1920s and 1930s, poor quality, insecure work and lack of progression would be the giant he would seek to slay.

We have argued throughout this book that underlying this crisis is the question of power and that the balance of power between low-paid workers and employers has shifted decisively towards the latter. People feel trapped: trapped by the lack of progression options but, most of all, trapped by the lack of alternative jobs that offer a better future. If there is no way out of your current workplace, and your employer knows that, what incentive do they have to try harder to keep you?

It seems fairly obvious that the state should have an interest in promoting good work, decent pay, and better progression. Higher tax revenues and a happier population are two of the obvious benefits. Moreover, social mobility has been a part of the political rhetoric of both the right and the left. On the face of it, therefore, there should be political unanimity on the mission to get the UK out of its rut. But rather than empowering its citizens, the truth is that the state – as it currently operates – is often part of the problem. We have shown how, time and again, in policy areas as diverse as unemployment, childcare, transport, and skills and regulation, the state conspires to constrain the labour supply of low-paid workers and reduce their power to have an alternative to their current employer.

The underlying problem in employment services, is an empirical question to which too many people seem to want to give an ideological answer. Is being out of work the fault of the people in question – i.e. down to their own "fecklessness" in some way – or is it a result of the circumstances – economic, health, geographical – in which they find themselves? Our employment services seem to be designed as if the first answer applies to most people. So we deliver an employment service that treats its recipients as if they are the problem to be managed, rather than part of the solution. Given that employment today is at historically high levels, this explanation is necessarily less true than it ever was. Once again, attitudes appear to be driven by the high unemployment levels that existed in the 1980s and early 1990s rather than the economic problems of today. Crucially, however, these attitudes do not just affect the dignity with which people out of work are treated. They also have a knock-on effect on power in the labour market. If the state's message is "take any job at any cost", employers know they have low-paid workers over a barrel.

This feeling of being trapped is exacerbated by poor infrastructure – childcare and transport services – that do not meet the needs of low-paid workers. Many low-paid jobs were crucial to our continued well-being during the pandemic lockdown. But we are no more likely after the pandemic to provide childcare services that meet the shift patterns of low-paid workers than we were before. Too often, public services such as these are not considered an essential part of economic policy despite their obvious effect on labour supply.

Despite high employment levels, employment gaps endure. Women, disabled people and people from ethnic minorities still experience high levels of disadvantage in the UK labour market. It goes without saying that this is unfair in its own right. It is also another example of constraints on labour supply that waste too much of the country's talent.

Economic orthodoxy doesn't help: traditional views on productivity and state regulation mean that the sorts of economic policies that would help low-paid workers and sectors don't happen, despite emerging evidence that these views are out of date. We see productivity policy confined to the shiny and new, and not the everyday economy where action could help low-paid workers as well as the economy as a whole. State regulation that might improve working conditions for the low-paid is assumed to be an economic negative, even when the evidence suggests this trade-off might not really exist.

Things could be different. But it requires real political ambition and turning on its head orthodoxies and established thinking on productivity, skills, active labour market policy and social infrastructure like childcare and transport.

As we have shown throughout this book, there are some encouraging signs: many businesses in low-paying sectors have made public commitments to pay the voluntary Real Living Wage; others have signed up to positive initiatives such as the Greater Manchester Good Employment Charter. Parts of the state – mostly devolved and city-region governments – have started to rise to the challenge of promoting better quality work. But these (largely voluntary) measures are not enough on their own to shift the UK towards a high-pay, high-productivity labour market.

WHAT WOULD A MORE PRODUCTIVE AND EMPOWERING APPROACH LOOK LIKE?

Throughout this book we have shown how the state creates far too many of the wrong incentives in its interaction with people out of work, pushing them into any job, however low quality and unlikely to lead to progression. "Work first" is a blunt model unsuitable for today's high employment labour market. Pushing people into any job regardless of fit or circumstance, it also fails to provide the tailored service needed for groups facing more significant barriers to work. This approach needs to change so that active labour market policies take a human capital approach – helping to build people up to a satisfying and productive career, not any job at any cost.

Moves towards a "work first, then work more" model for in-work claimants under Universal Credit simply involves an extension of the same old approach – intensifying pressure on people in low-paid, insecure work, to take more of the same, and which does nothing to address the UK's low-pay, low-productivity rut. We need a shift from a sanctions-based to a support-based system, one that empowers people to access quality opportunities and support genuine prospects for progression.

We shouldn't settle for a "nagging service". Jobcentres should be places people go to be inspired, where they can be supported to access quality opportunities in jobs that are both meaningful for them and productive for the economy as a whole. They might also usefully help to equip people with more knowledge about employment rights, leaving them less open to exploitation from employers, some of whom, as we have shown, continue to flout them. The key objective should not be moving people into any work, but to ensure that, where work is appropriate, people are supported into decent and productive work where their skills and capabilities will be developed and used effectively, and in which they can maximize their potential. To do this, policymakers must shift their priorities from short-term reductions in the benefits bill to aiming for a world-leading employment and skills service that will meet the needs of the labour market of the future.

Paying more attention to the kind of jobs people are moving into, and supporting people into work that is high quality and works well with people's needs and responsibilities outside of the paid labour market may cost more in the short term, but has higher payoffs for people, businesses and the economy in the long term. As in-work policy is developed, there should not be a narrow focus on getting people to increase their hours of work – it should instead be on helping people to access better hourly rates of pay, and work quality more generally. For some this might include thinking more holistically about progression – which may involve horizontal movement to jobs with better long-term prospects. The payoff for government in fiscal terms may take longer. However, the wider benefits: improvements in life satisfaction, well-being, health, and future pay prospects are likely to dwarf the fairly modest bill for this change.

Part of this means developing a skills system that works for people out of work and low-paid workers. The DWP needs to be an active contributor to people developing their skills and earning capacity, not its opponent. Importantly, if the state offers greater support to workers, rather than disempowering them, it can facilitate a more equitable balance of power between workers and employers, resulting in better terms of conditions and better pay.

RECOGNIZING THE ECONOMIC VALUE
OF TRANSPORT AND CHILDCARE

As we have seen, many of the issues that constrain the working lives of low-paid workers do not arise solely from active labour market policies. An unrealistic attitude to childcare, and a desperately poor local transport offer in many parts of the country, contribute to an environment in which labour market horizons often narrow when caring responsibilities intervene. The consequences are further constraints in the labour supply of low-paid women in particular, which enables employers to hold down wages and not to invest in development and progression. If we are realistic about liberating the UK's economy from its low-pay, low-productivity cycle, we must start treating services such as childcare and local transport as key economic infrastructure and not just social services.

The underlying problem is that policymaking is far too distant from the reality of low-paid working lives. Juggling childcare and shift work in sectors such as care, hospitality and retail is a long way from the corridors of Whitehall, and it shows. Low-paid work does not fit a simple 9 to 5 pattern and, if they are to be of use for low-paid workers, neither should transport and childcare services. Equally, Whitehall policymakers must not just consider the financing of childcare subsidies but make sure they get right issues of accessibility, availability and quality.

A starting point for better policymaking should be that reforms in relation to employment services, skills, childcare and transport should be shaped through greater involvement of

Universal Credit claimants, low-paid workers, employers, and unions – the very people who know about the realities of the labour market and who should be the intended beneficiaries of such policy changes.

IMPROVING WORK QUALITY
AND EMPLOYER PRACTICES

The need for widespread improvement in the quality of work available, including employer practices is perhaps the most critical need, and here government action has been weakest.

We have shown how an old-fashioned attitude that equates better labour market standards with higher business costs has led to a parsimonious attitude to regulation such that little action has been taken as legal and technological innovation has brushed aside several decades of employment protection. This old-fashioned view – that there is an equity vs efficiency trade-off – is wrong. This has been demonstrated comprehensively in relation to the minimum wage, substantially in relation to working hours and fairly strongly in many other areas. It is time for the government to start being proud of the UK being a place where, if you want to do business, labour standards are high. Not only will this improve the health and well-being of the population, but it is also likely to improve its wealth as productivity improves.

When politicians want to suggest they are focused on improving the economy, they like to say they are pro-business. But being pro-business is not the same as being pro-economy. For example, in the case of competition, being pro-economy means making it harder for businesses to create actual or quasi-monopolies. Being pro-economy needs to mean making businesses work harder to compete to attract their workers. That means shifting the balance of power so that workers – and particularly low-paid women – actually have the power, and believe they have the power, to pick and choose from the employers they see around them, rather than the other way around. This may seem difficult but it is essential if we wish to deliver pay rises for low-paid workers.

This means thinking actively about how to support low-paid workers to develop the skills for, and get, new jobs. Such support cannot in principle be delivered through the current employer – the whole point is to widen choices beyond the current employer. So government needs to think creatively about job brokerages and skills support delivered through other means if it wants to redress the power imbalance in the workplace.

In addition much more emphasis should be placed on improving employer practices, rather than citizen behaviour. Government needs to do more to both support and require employers to be better businesses and, crucially, better managers. Some of this – but by no means all – can be delivered by restoring to every employee employment protections (such as the right to a meaningful contract of employment) that we should take for granted. However, government also has power through its procurement rules and its convening power to improve the quality of work. This is happening at some levels of government in some places, but it needs to be more widespread, and operate at a national level.

CHANGING ECONOMICS AND
ECONOMIC POLICY FOR THE BETTER

Critically, economics needs to reject the notion that, in the short term, workers have a fixed level of productivity. This ignores a mountain of evidence, and much real-life experience, that management matters. In particular, efforts need to be directed at management outside of the country's small proportion of frontier firms. This entails thinking about management education, and support for small businesses in a completely different way.

This is a hard ask, but there have been successful pilots such as Be the Business and the CIPD People Skills project that have shown the way, and some recent Chancellors of the Exchequer have become alive to the question of management. But the conversation has only just started. It will require a radical change in economic and work culture for good management to become something to be proud of, to aspire to, and be prepared to spend time and money on learning to be good at. The government cannot be the only actor here, but it does have the convening power to stimulate and accelerate the process. If we get this right, we have the prospect of making a real difference to the productivity of the nation as a whole, and creating an environment that is more likely to provide higher quality work to many more people.

If the Beveridge Report was about anything, it was about not tinkering around the edges and that big challenges have to be faced. A high pay high productivity economy will not be achieved through rhetoric. To lift the UK out of its low-pay, low-productivity rut requires similarly bold thinking, to which we hope this book has made a contribution.

References

Abreu, M. 2020. "Human capital, skills and productivity". In P. McCann & T. Vorley (eds), *Productivity Perspectives*, 174–89. Cheltenham: Elgar.

Adler, M. 2018. *Cruel, Inhuman or Degrading Treatment? Benefit Sanctions in the UK*. Basingstoke: Palgrave Macmillan.

Age UK 2017. "5 million grandparents take on childcare responsibilities". https://www.ageuk.org.uk/latest-news/articles/2017/september/five-million-grandparents-take-on-childcare-responsibilities/.

Alakeson, V., M. Brewer & D. Finch 2015. "Credit where it's due? Assessing the benefits and risks of Universal Credit". London: Resolution Foundation. https://www.resolutionfoundation.org/publications/credit-where-its-due-assessing-the-benefits-and-risks-of-universal-credit/.

Aldridge, F. & D. Hughes 2012. *NIACE Adult Participation in Learning Survey*. Leicester: National Institute for Adult Continuing Education.

Alston, P. 2018. Report of the Special Rapporteur on Extreme Poverty and Human Rights on His Mission to the United States of America". United Nations General Assembly.

Ames, C. 2020. "Liverpool city region set to back bus franchising". The Transport Network, 20 February. https://www.transport-network.co.uk/Liverpool-city-region-set-to-back-bus-franchising/16465.

Andersen, K. 2020. "Universal Credit, gender and unpaid childcare: Mothers' accounts of the new welfare conditionality regime". *Critical Social Policy* 40(3): 430–49.

Assinder, N. 1998. "Minimum wage leads to cabinet rift". BBC News. http://news.bbc.co.uk/1/hi/uk_politics/115193.stm.

Atkinson, C., B. Lupton & L. Crowley 2019. "Productivity and place: the role of LEPs in raising the demand for, and use of, skills at work". https://www.cipd.co.uk/Images/productivity-and-place-the-role-of-leps-v2_tcm18-54430.pdf.

Barnard, H. *et al.* 2017. *UK Poverty 2017*. York: Joseph Rowntree Foundation. https://www.jrf.org.uk/report/uk-poverty-2017.

Baumberg Geiger, B. 2018. "A better WCA is possible". London: Demos. https://demosuk.wpengine.com/wp-content/uploads/2018/02/2018_A_Better_WCA_is_possible_FULL-4.pdf.

BBC News 2015. "Chancellor opens National Graphene Institute in Manchester". BBC News. https://www.bbc.co.uk/news/uk-england-manchester-31996018.

Beatty, C. & S. Fothergill 2005. "The diversion from 'unemployment' to 'sickness' across British regions and districts". *Regional Studies* 39(7): 837–54.

Becker, E., O. Hayllar & M. Wood 2010. "Pathways to work: programme engagement and work patterns". London: Department for Work and Pensions.

BEIS 2017. "Industrial strategy: building a Britain fit for the future". Cm9528. https://bit.ly/302zeNe

BEIS 2018. "Good work plan". https://www.gov.uk/government/publications/good-work-plan.

BEIS 2021. "Establishing a new single enforcement body for employment rights: government response". London.

Bennett, H. 2017a. "Collaborative inquiry exploring data and knowledge-sharing practices in responses to welfare sanctions". University of Edinburgh/What Works Scotland.

Bennett, H. 2017b. "Re-examining British welfare-to-work contracting using a transaction cost perspective". *Journal of Social Policy* 46(1): 129–48.

Beveridge, W. 1942. *Social Insurance and Allied Services*. London: HMSO.

Bhattacharya, A., S. Corfe & A. Norman 2020. *Adult Education, Education, Education: How Adult Education Can Improve the Life Chances of Those On Low Incomes*. York: Joseph Rowntree Foundation/Social Market Foundation. https://www.smf.co.uk/wp-content/uploads/2020/11/Adult-education-education-education-Nov-2020.pdf.

BIS 2014. "The Impact of the Working Time Regulations on the UK labour market: A review of evidence". BIS Analysis Paper No. 5. London: BIS. https://assets.publishing.service.gov.uk/government/uploads/system/uploads/attachment_data/file/389676/bis-14-1287-the-impact-of-the-working-time-regulations-on-the-uk-labour-market-a-review-of-evidence.pdf.

Blanchflower, D. & A. Posen 2014. "Wages and labor market slack:

making the dual mandate operational". Working Paper WP 14–6. Washington, DC: Peterson Institute for International Economics. https://www.piie.com/publications/wp/wp14-6.pdf.

Bloom, N. & J. Van Reenen 2007. "Measuring and explaining management practices across firms and countries". *Quarterly Journal of Economics* 122(4): 1351–408.

Bloom, N., R. Sadun & J. Van Reenen 2017. "Management as a technology?" CEP Discussion Paper No 1433. London: Centre for Economic Performance. https://cep.lse.ac.uk/pubs/download/dp1433.pdf.

Bloy, M. n.d. "Factory Legislation 1802–1878". A Web of English History. http://www.historyhome.co.uk/peel/factmine/factleg.htm.

Boeren, E. 2016. *Lifelong Learning Participation in a Changing Policy Context: An Interdisciplinary Theory*. Berlin: Springer.

Boeren, E. 2019. "Being an adult learner in Europe and the UK: persisting inequalities and the role of the Welfare State". In E. Boeren & N. James (eds), *Being an Adult Learner in Austere Times*. London: Palgrave Macmillan.

Boswell, J. *et al.* 2018. *Making Ends Meet: The Lived Experience of Poverty in the South*. Southampton: Southern Policy Centre. https://southernpolicycentre.co.uk/wp-content/uploads/2018/06/Making-Ends-Meet-full-report-draft.pdf.

Bosworth, D. & C. Warhurst 2020. "Does good work have a positive effect on productivity? Developing the evidence base". In Carnegie/RSA (eds), *Can Good Work Solve the Productivity Puzzle?* https://www.thersa.org/globalassets/reports/2020/can-good-work-solve-the-productivity-puzzle.pdf.

Bound, H. *et al.* 2018. *How Non-Permanent Workers Learn and Develop: Challenges and Opportunities*. Abingdon: CRC Press.

Boxall, P., M.-L. Huo & J. Winterton 2019. "How do workers benefit from skill utilisation and how can these benefits be enhanced?" *Journal of Industrial Relations* 61(5): 704–25.

Brewer, M. & A. Shephard 2004. *Has Labour Made Work Pay?* York: Joseph Rowntree Foundation. https://discovery.ucl.ac.uk/id/eprint/18462/1/18462.pdf.

Brewer, M., D. Finch & D. Tomlinson 2017. *Universal Remedy: Ensuring Universal Credit Is Fit For Purpose*. London: Resolution Foundation. https://www.resolutionfoundation.org/app/uploads/2017/10/Universal-Credit.pdf.

Briken, K. & P. Taylor 2018. "Fulfilling the 'British way': beyond constrained choice – Amazon workers' lived experiences of workfare". *Industrial Relations Journal* 49(5/6): 438–58.

Britton, J. *et al.* 2020. *2020 Annual Report on Education Spending in England*. Institute for Fiscal Studies. https://ifs.org.uk/uploads/ R182-2020-annual-report-on-education-spending-in-England.pdf.

Bureau of Labor Statistics 2021. "The employment situation – November 2021". Washington, DC: US Department of Labor. https://www.bls.gov/news.release/archives/empsit_12032021.pdf.

Butler, S. 2021. "Supreme Court rules against Asda in workers' equal pay case". *The Guardian*, 16 March. https://www.theguardian.com/ business/2021/mar/26/court-rules-against-asda-in-workers-equal-pay-case.

Card, D., J. Kluve & A. Weber 2015. "What works? A meta-analysis of recent active labour market program evaluations". IZA DP No. 9236.

Carson, C. 2021. "5 Employer experiences of the living wage in the higher education, hospitality and construction sectors". In T. Dobbins & P. Prowse (eds), *The Living Wage: Advancing a Global Movement*, 52–64. Abingdon: Routledge.

Carter, E. & A. Whitworth 2015. "Creaming and parking in quasi-marketised welfare-to-work schemes: designed out of or designed in to the UK work programme?" *Journal of Social Policy* 44(2): 277–96.

Centre for Social Justice 2009. *Dynamic Benefits: Towards Welfare That Works*. London: CSJ. https://www.centreforsocialjustice.org.uk/ library/dynamic-benefits-towards-welfare-that-works.

CIPD 2015. "Zero-hours and short-hours contracts in the UK: employer and employee perspectives". London: CIPD. https://www.cipd. co.uk/Images/zero-hours-and-short-hours-contracts-in-the-uk_ 2015-employer-employee-perspectives_tcm18-10713.pdf.

CIPD 2017. *An Evaluation of HR Business Support Pilots People Skills*. London.

Citizens Advice 2015. *Neither One Thing Nor the Other: How Reducing Bogus Self-employment Could Benefit Workers, Business and the Exchequer*. https://www.citizensadvice.org.uk/Global/ CitizensAdvice/Work%20Publications/Neither%20one%.

Clarke, J. 1944. *Social Security Guide: The White Paper and the Beveridge Report Compared*. London: Social Security League. https://wdc. contentdm.oclc.org/digital/collection/health/id/1169.

Clasen, J. & D. Clegg 2011. *Regulating the Risk of Unemployment: National Adaptations to Post-Industrial Labour Markets in Europe*. Oxford: Oxford University Press.

Clasen, J. 2020. "Subsidizing wages or supplementing transfers? The politics and ambiguity of in-work benefits". *Social Policy & Administration* 54(1): 1–13.

Clegg, D. 2015. "The demise of tax credits". *Political Quarterly* 86(4): 493–9.

Cominetti, N. 2020. *Calculating the Real Living Wage for London and the Rest of the UK: 2020–21*. London: Resolution Foundation. https://www.resolutionfoundation.org/publications/calculating-the-real-living-wage-for-london-and-the-rest-of-the-uk/.

Cominetti, N. & L. Judge 2019. *From Rights to Reality: Enforcing Labour Market Laws in the UK*. London: Resolution Foundation. https://www.resolutionfoundation.org/publications/from-rights-to-reality/.

Cominetti, N., C. McCurdy & H. Slaughter 2021. *Low Pay Britain 2021*. London: Resolution Foundation. https://www.resolutionfoundation.org/publications/low-pay-britain-2021/.

Conservative Party 2010. "The Conservative Manifesto 2010: Invitation to Join the Government of Britain". London: Conservative Party. https://conservativehome.blogs.com/files/conservative-manifesto-2010.pdf.

Cribb, J. *et al.* 2017. *In-work Poverty Among Families with Children*. London: IFS. https://ifs.org.uk/uploads/publications/comms/r129_ch5.pdf.

Danker, T. 2020. "Productivity through people – supporting best practice in SMEs". In Carnegie/RSA (eds), *Can Good Work Solve the Productivity Puzzle?*

Daycare Trust 2008. *Childcare Costs Survey 2008*. London: Daycare Trust. https://www.familyandchildcaretrust.org/sites/default/files/Resource%20Library/Cost_survey2008.pdf.

Denman, J. & P. McDonald 1996. "Unemployment statistics from 1881 to the present day". Labour Market Trends, January 1996: 5–18. London: ONS. https://escoe-website.s3.amazonaws.com/wp-content/uploads/2018/10/17145130/Denman-and-Macdonald-LMT-1996-Unemployment-Statistics-from-1881-to-the-present-day.pdf.

Dewar, L. & E. Clery 2020. *Left Behind: Single Parents with Pre-School Aged Children and Job-seeking Under Universal Credit in London*. London: Gingerbread.

DfE 2019. *Childcare and Early Years Survey of Parents in England, 2019*. London. https://www.gov.uk/government/statistics/childcare-and-early-years-survey-of-parents-2019.

DfE 2020. *Employer Skills Survey 2019: Skills Needs Research Report*. https://assets.publishing.service.gov.uk/government/uploads/system/uploads/attachment_data/file/936489/ESS_2019_Skills_Needs_Report_Nov20.pdf.

DfE 2021. *Skills For Jobs: Lifelong Learning for Opportunity and Growth*. https://www.gov.uk/government/publications/skills-for-jobs-lifelong-learning-for-opportunity-and-growth.

DfE/DWP 2019. *Further Education for Benefit Claimants, England, 2017/18 Academic Year*. https://assets.publishing.service.gov.uk/government/uploads/system/uploads/attachment_data/file/835749/Further_Education_for_Benefit_Claimants.pdf.

DfT 2021a. *Bus Back Better: National BUS Strategy for England*. London.

DfT 2021b. *Costs, Fares and Revenue BUS04*. https://www.gov.uk/government/statistical-data-sets/bus04-costs-fares-and-revenue.

DfT 2021c. Local Bus passenger journeys BUS01. Bus Statistics. https://www.gov.uk/government/statistical-data-sets/bus01-local-bus-passenger-journeys#table-bus0103.

DfT 2021d. Travel by household quintile and main mode or mode: England NTS0705. Mode of Travel. https://www.gov.uk/government/statistical-data-sets/nts03-modal-comparisons.

Dromey, J., L. Dewar & J. Finnegan 2020. *Tackling Single Parent Poverty After Coronavirus*. London: Learning and Work Institute. https://www.gingerbread.org.uk/wp-content/uploads/2020/12/Tackling-single-parent-poverty-after-coronavirus.pdf.

Dube, A. 2019. *Impacts of Minimum Wages: Review of the International Evidence*. London: HM Treasury.

DWP 2007. *In Work, Better Off: Next Steps to Full Employment*. Cmd 7130. London.

DWP 2008. *DWP Commissioning Strategy*. Cmd 7330. London.

DWP 2010. *Universal Credit: Welfare that Works*. Cmd 7957. London.

DWP 2016. *Sector-based Work Academies: A Quantitative Impact Assessment*. https://assets.publishing.service.gov.uk/government/uploads/system/uploads/attachment_data/file/508175/rr918-sector-based-work-academies.pdf.

DWP 2017. *Understanding How Universal Credit Influences Employment Behaviour: Findings From Qualitative and Experimental Research With Claimants*. https://assets.publishing.service.gov.uk/government/uploads/system/uploads/attachment_data/file/643952/understanding-how-universal-credit-influences-employment-behaviour.pdf.

DWP 2018a. *Employer Guide to Universal Credit*. London: DWP.

DWP 2018b. *Universal Credit: In-Work Progression Randomised Controlled Trial*. London: DWP.

DWP 2020. *Universal Credit: Health Conditions and Disability Guide*. https://www.gov.uk/government/publications/universal-credit-

if-you-have-a-disability-or-health-condition-quick-guide/
universal-credit-if-you-have-a-disability-or-health-condition.

DWP 2021a. *The Future Cohort Study: Understanding Universal Credit's Future In-Work Claimant Group.* London: DWP.

DWP 2021b. *Shaping Future Support: The Health and Disability Green Paper.* London: DWP.

DWP/BIS 2010. *Skills Conditionality: Public Consultation.* London: HM Government.

DWP/BIS 2011. *Skills Conditionality: Government Response to the Consultation.*

Dwyer, P. & S. Wright 2014. "Universal Credit, ubiquitous conditionality and its implications for social citizenship". *Journal of Poverty and Social Justice* 22(1): 27.

Dwyer, P. *et al.* 2018. "Final findings: disabled people". Welfare Conditionality: Sanctions, Support and Behaviour Change. http://www.welfareconditionality.ac.uk/wp-content/uploads/2018/05/40414-Disabled-people-web.pdf.

Dwyer, P., *et al.* 2020. "Work, welfare, and wellbeing: the impacts of welfare conditionality on people with mental health impairments in the UK". *Social Policy & Administration* 54(2): 311–26.

Dwyer, P. *et al.* forthcoming. *The Impacts of Welfare Conditionality: Sanctions Support and Behaviour Change.* Bristol: Policy Press.

Etherington, D. & J. Ingold 2012. "Welfare to work and the inclusive labour market: a comparative study of activation policies for disability and long-term sickness benefit claimants in the UK and Denmark". *Journal of European Social Policy* 22(1): 30–44.

Evans, S. & J. Dromey 2020. *Coronavirus and the Labour Market: Impacts and Challenges.* Leicester: Learning and Work Institute.

Fitzgerald, T. 2015. "Chinese President visits Manchester: Xi Jinping tours University's National Graphene Institute". *Manchester Evening News.* https://www.manchestereveningnews.co.uk/news/greater-manchester-news/chinese-president-visits-manchester-xi-10320402.

Fitzpatrick, S. *et al.* 2020. *Destitution in the UK 2020.* York: Joseph Rowntree Foundation.

Fletcher, D. & S. Wright 2018. "A hand up or a slap down? Criminalising benefit claimants in Britain via strategies of surveillance, sanctions and deterrence". *Critical Social Policy* 38(2): 323–44.

Foreign and Commonwealth Office 2018. *Women and the Foreign Office: A History.* London History Notes.

Freud, D. 2007. *Reducing Dependency, Increasing Opportunity: Options for the Future of Welfare to Work.* London: DWP.

Freud, D. 2021. *Clashing Agendas: Inside the Welfare Trap*. London: Nine Elms Books.

Gable, O. 2021. "Millions on Universal Credit face barriers to accessing training". Lancaster: The Work Foundation. https://www.lancaster.ac.uk/work-foundation/news/blog/millions-on-universal-credit-face-barriers-to-accessing-training.

Gales, K. & P. Marks 1974. "Twentieth-century trends in the work of women in England and Wales". *Journal of the Royal Statistical Society* 137(1): 60–74.

Gardiner, L. 2015. *The Scale of Minimum Wage Underpayment in Social Care*. London: Resolution Foundation. https://www.resolution foundation.org/app/uploads/2015/02/NMW-social-care-note1.pdf.

Garthwaite, K. 2014. "Fear of the brown envelope: exploring welfare reform with long-term sickness benefits recipients". *Social Policy & Administration* 48(7): 782–98.

Green, A. 2021. "The Covid-19 crisis and implications for skills development and the skills system". In P. McCann & T. Vorley (eds), *Productivity and the Pandemic*. Cheltenham: Elgar.

Green, A. *et al.* 2018. *Raising Productivity in Low-Wage Sectors and Reducing Poverty*. York: Joseph Rowntree Foundation.

Griggs, J. & M. Evans 2010. *Sanctions Within Conditional Benefit Systems: A Review of Evidence*. York: Joseph Rowntree Foundation

Grogger, J. & L. Karoly 2005. *Welfare Reform: Effects of a Decade of Change*. Cambridge, MA: Harvard University Press.

Grunfeld, C. 1964. "Contracts of Employment Act, 1963". *Modern Law Review* 27(1): 70–80.

Haapanala, H. 2021. "Carrots or sticks? A multilevel analysis of active labour market policies and non-standard employment in Europe". *Social Policy & Administration* 56(3): 360–77.

Haldane, A. 2018. *The UK's Productivity Problem: Hub No Spokes*. London: Bank of England.

Haldane, A. 2017. *Productivity Puzzles*. London: Bank of England.

Hansard HC Deb. vol 308 cols 145–6, 9 March 1998.

Hansard HC Deb. vol 318 cols 219–20, 27 October 1998.

Hansard HC Deb. vol 598 col. 337, 8 July 2015.

Hansard HC Deb. vol 656 col. 349, 13 March 2019.

Hasluck, C. & A. Green 2007. "What works for whom?" Corporate Document Services.

Heery, E., D. Nash & D. Hann 2017. "The Living Wage employer experience". Cardiff Business School, Cardiff. www.cardiff.ac.uk/_data/assets/pdf_file/0008/722429/The-Living-Wage-Employer-Experience-Report.pdf.

Heins, E. & H. Bennett 2018. "Retrenchment, conditionality and flexibility: UK labour market policies in the era of austerity". In S. Theodoropoulou (ed.) *Labour Market Policies in the Era of Pervasive Austerity*. Bristol: Policy Press.

Hemming, M., B. Fall & U. O'Shea 1965. "Social security in Britain and certain other countries". *National Institute Economic Review* 33(1): 48–67.

Hendra, R. *et al.* 2016. *Encouraging Evidence on a Sector-Focused Advancement Strategy: Two-Year Impacts*. WorkAdvance Demonstration.

Henehan, K. 2021. *Uneven Steps: Changes in Youth Unemployment and Study Since the Onset of Covid-19*. London: The Resolution Foundation. https://www.resolutionfoundation.org/publications/uneven-steps/.

HM Treasury 2015a. *Summer Budget 2015*. London: HM Treasury.

HM Treasury 2015b. *Fixing the Foundations: Creating a More Prosperous Nation*. London: HM Treasury.

House of Commons Liaison Committee (2021) Oral evidence from the Prime Minister, HC 491 Wednesday 7 July 2021. https://committees.parliament.uk/oralevidence/2308/default/.

HSE 2020. Costs to Britain of workplace fatalities and self-reported injuries and ill health, 2018/19.

HSE 2021. Historical picture statistics in Great Britain, 2021. https://www.hse.gov.uk/statistics/history/historical-picture.pdf.

Hughes, C. *et al.* 2017. *Good Jobs in Greater Manchester: The Role of Employment Charters*. https://oxfamilibrary.openrepository.com/handle/10546/620251.

Iglikowski, V. 2015. "'A perfect nuisance': the history of women in the Civil Service". https://history.blog.gov.uk/2015/05/26/a-perfect-nuisance-the-history-of-women-in-the-civil-service/.

Illeris, K. 2006. "What is special about adult learning?". In P. Sutherland & J. Crowther (eds), *Lifelong Learning: Concepts and Contexts*. London: Routledge.

Incomes Data Research 2018. *Minimum and Zero Hours Contracts and Low-paid Staff*. London: Low Pay Commission.

Innes, D. 2018. *The Links Between Low Productivity, Low Pay and In-Work Poverty*. York: Joseph Rowntree Foundation.

Innes, D. 2020. *What Has Driven the Rise of In-Work Poverty?* York: Joseph Rowntree Foundation.

Institute of Employment Rights 2021. "New Director of Labour Market Enforcement appointed". https://www.ier.org.uk/news/new-director-of-labour-market-enforcement-appointed/.

ILO 1944. International Labour Conference: Declaration Concerning
    the Aims and Purposes of the International Labour Organisation.
    Geneva: International Labour Organization. https://www.ilo.org/
    global/about-the-ilo/newsroom/news/WCMS_698995/lang--en/
    index.htm.

ILO 2019. *Quick Guide on Interpreting the Unemployment Rate*. Geneva:
    ILO.

Irvine, G., D. White & M. Diffley 2018. *Measuring Good Work*.
    Dunfermline: Carnegie UK Trust. https://www.thersa.org/
    globalassets/reports/2020/can-good-work-solve-the-
    productivity-puzzle.pdf.

James, N. & E. Boeren (eds) 2019. *Being an Adult Learner in Austere Times*.
    London: Palgrave Macmillan.

Jarvie, M., S. Shorto & H. Parlett 2021. *Childcare Survey 2021*. London.

Johnsen, S. & J. Blenkinsopp 2018. "Final findings: lone parents". Welfare
    Conditionality: Sanctions, Support and Behaviour Change.

Johnson, D. & P. Mackie 2013. *Buses and the Economy II: Survey of Bus Use
    Amongst the Unemployed*. Leeds: University of Leeds.

Jones, K. 2019. "'I've always been a grafter': Older benefit recipients and
    welfare conditionality". *Journal of Social Security Law* 25(3): 173–86.

Jones, K. 2021a. "Active labour market policy in a post-Covid UK:
    moving beyond a work first approach". In *Productivity and the
    Pandemic*.

Jones, K. 2021b. "Understanding adult education in community
    contexts: a critical realist perspective". *British Educational Research
    Journal* 47(3): 674–91.

Jones, K. 2022. "Heads in the sand: the absence of employers in new
    developments in UK active labour market policy". *Political Quarterly*
    93(2): 253–60.

Jones, K. *et al.* 2019. *Universal Credit and In-Work Conditionality:
    A Productive Turn?* Productivity Insights Network.

Jones, K., P. Martin & A. Kelly 2018. "Hidden young people in Salford:
    exploring the experiences of young people not in employment,
    education or training NEET and not claiming benefits". University
    of Salford.

Joyce, R. & A. Keiller 2018. "The 'gender commuting gap' widens
    considerably in the first decade after childbirth". Institute for Fiscal
    Studies. https://www.ifs.org.uk/publications/13673.

Judge, L. & A. Stansbury 2020. *Under the Wage Floor: Exploring Firms'
    Incentives to Comply with the Minimum Wage*. London: Resolution
    Foundation.

Kaufman, J. 2020. "Intensity, moderation, and the pressures of expectation: calculation and coercion in the street-level practice of welfare conditionality". *Social Policy & Administration* 54(2): 205–18.

King's College London & Working Families 2021. *Working Parents, Flexibility and Job Quality: What Are the Trade-offs?* https://workingfamilies.org.uk/wp-content/uploads/2021/11/Working-parents-flexibility-and-job-quality-what-are-the-trade-offs.pdf.

Kumar, A., M. Rotik & K. Ussher 2014. *Pay Progression: Understanding the Barriers for the Lowest Paid.* London. https://www.cipd.co.uk/knowledge/fundamentals/people/pay/progression-barriers-report.

Labour Party 1996. *New Labour Because Britain Deserves Better: Labour Party Manifesto, General Election 1997.* https://web.archive.org/web/20110927045458/http://www.politicsresources.net/area/uk/man/lab97.htm.

Lane, M. & G. Conlon 2016. "The impact of literacy, numeracy and computer skills on earnings and employment outcomes". OECD Education Working Papers No. 129. Paris: OECD Publishing.

Lee, N. & S. Clarke 2019. "Do low-skilled workers gain from high-tech employment growth? High-technology multipliers, employment and wages in Britain". *Research Policy* 48(9): 103803.

Lindsay, C., R. McQuaid & M. Dutton 2007. "New approaches to employability in the UK: combining 'human capital development' and 'work first' strategies?" *Journal of Social Policy* 36(4): 539–60.

Lindsay, C. *et al.* 2018. "Co-production as a route to employability: lessons from services with lone parents". *Public Administration* 96(2): 318–32.

Living Wage Foundation 2021. *Accredited Living Wage Employers.* https://www.livingwage.org.uk/accredited-living-wage-employers.

Low Pay Commission 2015. *National Minimum Wage: Low Pay Commission Report 2015.* Cm 9017. London.

Low Pay Commission 2020. *Low Pay Commission 2020 Report.* https://assets.publishing.service.gov.uk/government/uploads/system/uploads/attachment_data/file/942062/LPC_Report_2020.pdf.

Low Pay Commission 2021. *Non-compliance and Enforcement of the National Minimum Wage.* London.

Luby, J. & J. Welch 2006. *Missed Opportunities: The Case for Investment in Learning and Skills for Homeless People.* London: Crisis.

Maguire, K. 2019. "Zero hours contracts: a short-term fix, but not a long-term strategy". HR Zone. https://www.hrzone.com/talent/acquisition/zero-hours-contracts-a-short-term-fix-but-not-a-long-term-strategy.

McCarthy, H. 2014. "Women, marriage and work in the British Diplomatic Service". *Women's History Review* 23(6): 853–73.

McGregor-Smith, R. 2021. *Supporting Progression Out of Low Pay: A Call to Action*. London: DWP.

Mead, L. 1992. *The New Politics of Poverty*. New York: Basic Books.

Merrick, R. 2020. "'Cover-up': DWP destroyed reports into people who killed themselves after benefits were stopped". *Independent*, 26 February. https://www.independent.co.uk/news/uk/politics/dwp-benefit-death-suicide-reports-cover-ups-government-conservatives-a9359606.html.

Metcalf, D. 1999. "The Low Pay Commission and the National Minimum Wage". *Economic Journal* 109(453).

Millar, J. & F. Bennett 2017. "Universal Credit: assumptions, contradictions and virtual reality". *Social Policy and Society* 16(2): 169–82.

Moore, S. *et al.* 2018. "'Fits and fancies': the Taylor Review, the construction of preference and labour market segmentation". *Industrial Relations Journal* 49(5/6): 403–19.

Murray, C. 1984. *Losing Ground*. New York: Harper Collins.

NAO 2013. *Universal Credit: Early Progress*. London.

NAO 2016. *Benefit Sanctions*. HC 628.

Newton, B. *et al.* 2020. *Supporting Disadvantaged Young People into Meaningful Work: An Initial Evidence Review to Identify What Works and Inform Good Practice Among Practitioners and Employers*. Brighton: Institute for Employment Studies.

Nickell, S. & Saleheen, J. (2015) *The impact of immigration on occupational wages: evidence from Britain*. Bank of England Staff Working Paper No. 574. London: Bank of England. https://www.bankofengland.co.uk/working-paper/2015/the-impact-of-immigration-on-occupational-wages-evidence-from-britain.

O'Grady, A. & C. Atkin 2006. "Choosing to learn or chosen to learn: the experience of Skills for Life learners". *Research in Post-Compulsory Education* 11: 277–87.

OBR 2015. *Economic and Fiscal Outlook July 2015*. London: Office for Budget Responsibility.

OBR 2022. *Economic and Fiscal Outlook March 2022*. London: Office for Budget Responsibility.

OECD 2021a. *OECD Data: Employment Rate*. https://data.oecd.org/emp/employment-rate.htm.

OECD 2021b. *Productivity Statistics*. https://stats.oecd.org/Index.aspx?DataSetCode=PDB_LV.

OECD 2022. *Benefits in Unemployment, Share of Previous Income*. https://data.oecd.org/benwage/benefits-in-unemployment-share-of-previous-income.htm.

Olisa, J., J. Patterson & F. Wright 2010. *Turning the Key: Portraits of Low*

Literacy Amongst People with Experience of Homelessness. London: Thames Reach.

ONS 2019. "Analysis of job changers and stayers". https://www.ons.gov. uk/economy/nationalaccounts/uksectoraccounts/compendium/ economicreview/april2019/analysisofjobchangersandstayers.

ONS 2020. "Firm-level labour productivity measures from the Annual Business Survey, Great Britain". https://www.ons.gov.uk/economy/ economicoutputandproductivity/productivitymeasures/articles/ firmlevellabourproductivitymeasuresfromtheannualbusiness surveygreatbritain/1998to2018.

ONS 2021a. "Annual survey of hours and earnings, time series of selected estimates". https://www.ons.gov.uk/employmentand labourmarket/peopleinwork/earningsandworkinghours/datasets/ ashe1997to2015selectedestimates.

ONS 2021b. "Gender pay gap in the UK: 2021". https://www.ons.gov. uk/employmentandlabourmarket/peopleinwork/earningsand workinghours/bulletins/genderpaygapintheuk/2021.

ONS 2021c. "People in employment on zero hours contracts – Dataset". https://www.ons.gov.uk/employmentandlabourmarket/ peopleinwork/employmentandemployeetypes/datasets/ emp17peopleinemploymentonzerohourscontracts.

ONS 2021d. "Employment rates of people by parental status: Table P. Working and workless households in the UK". https://www.ons. gov.uk/employmentandlabourmarket/peopleinwork/employment andemployeetypes/datasets/workingandworklesshousehold stablepemploymentratesofpeoplebyparentalstatus.

ONS 2022. "International comparisons of UK productivity, final estimates: 2020". https://www.ons.gov.uk/economy/ economicoutputandproductivity/productivitymeasures/bulletins/ internationalcomparisonsofproductivityfinalestimates/2020.

Osikominu, A. 2021. "The dynamics of training programs for the unemployed". *IZA World of Labor* 277(2). doi:10.15185/izawol. 277.v2.

Osterman, P. 2013. "Introduction to the special issue on job quality: what does it mean and how might we think about it?" *Industrial and Labor Relations Review* 66(4): 739–52.

Pollard, T. 2018. *Pathways from Poverty: A Case for Institutional Reform*. London: Demos.

Raikes, L. 2019. *Transport Investment in the Northern Powerhouse: 2019 Update*. Manchester: IPPR North. https://www.ippr.org/files/ 2019-08/transport-investment-in-the-northern-powerhouse- august19.pdf.

Ray, K. *et al.* 2014. *Employment, Pay and Poverty: An Evidence Review*. York: Joseph Rowntree Foundation.

Recruiting Times 2017. "Are short-hour contracts the new zero-hour contracts?" *Recruiting Times*. https://recruitingtimes.org/opinions/19386/short-hour-contracts-new-zero-hour-contracts/.

Reder, S. 2009. "The development of literacy and numeracy in adult life". In S. Reder & J. Bynner (eds), *Tracking Adult Literacy and Numeracy Skills: Findings from Longitudinal Research*. Abingdon: Routledge.

Reeves, A. 2017. "Does sanctioning disabled claimants of unemployment insurance increase labour market inactivity? An analysis of 346 British local authorities between 2009 and 2014". *Journal of Poverty and Social Justice* 25(2): 129–46.

Reeves, A. *et al.* 2022. "Does capping social security harm health? A natural experiment in the UK". *Social Policy & Administration* 56(3): 345–59.

Roantree, B. & K. Vira 2018. "The rise and rise of women's employment in the UK". London IFS Briefing Note.

Rolfe, H. 2012. "Requiring the long-term unemployed to train: is benefit conditionality effective?" *National Institute Economic Review* 219: R65–76.

Romei, V. & J. Conboye 2019. "Lone parents face a challenge to stay in work". *Financial Times*. https://www.ft.com/content/c6ac954a-5c6a-11e9-9dde-7aedca0a081a.

Rose, E. *et al.* 2017. "Inaccessible justice: what happens to workers who don't pursue employment claims?" University of Strathclyde. https://pureportal.strath.ac.uk/en/publications/inaccessible-justice-what-happens-to-workers-who-dont-pursue-empl.

Rubery, J. *et al.* 2018. "Challenges and contradictions in the 'normalising' of precarious work". *Work, Employment and Society* 32(3): 509–27.

Rudd, A. 2019. "The future of the labour market". Speech. London: Department for Work and Pensions. https://www.gov.uk/government/speeches/the-future-of-the-labour-market.

Ryan, F. 2020. *Crippled: Austerity and the Demonization of Disabled People*. London: Verso.

Sainsbury, R. & K. Weston 2010. *Exploratory Qualitative Research on the Single Working Age Benefit*. DWP Research Report.

Sayce, L. 2018. *Switching Focus: Whose Responsibility to Improve Disabled People's Employment and Pay*. York: Joseph Rowntree Foundation.

Scholz, F. & J. Ingold 2021. "Activating the 'ideal jobseeker': experiences of individuals with mental health conditions on the UK Work Programme". *Human Relations* 74(10): 1604–27.

Scullion, L. *et al.* 2019. *Sanctions, Support and Service Leavers: Social Security Benefits, Welfare Conditionality and Transitions from Military to Civilian Life: Final Report*. Forces in Mind Trust.

Scullion, L. & K. Curchin 2022. "Examining veterans' interactions with the UK social security system through a trauma-informed lens". *Journal of Social Policy* 51(1): 96–113.

Sissons, P. 2020. *Making Progress? The Challenges and Opportunities for Increasing Wage and Career Progression*. London: The Work Foundation.

Sissons, P. & A. Green 2017. "More than a match? Assessing the HRM challenge of engaging employers to support retention and progression". *Human Resource Management Journal* 27(4): 565–80.

Sissons, P. & K. Jones 2016. "Local industrial strategy and skills policy in England: assessing the linkages and limitations – a case study of the Sheffield City Deal". *Local Economy* 31: 857–72.

Social Exclusion Unit 2003. *Making the Connections: Final Report on Transport and Social Exclusion*. London.

Spielhofer, T. *et al.* 2008. *Barriers to Participation in Education and Training*. London: Department for Education. https://assets. publishing.service.gov.uk/government/uploads/system/uploads/ attachment_data/file/182518/DFE-RR009.pdf.

SSAC 2017. "In-work progression and Universal Credit: a study by the Social Security Advisory Committee". Occasional Paper No. 19. https://assets.publishing.service.gov.uk/government/uploads/ system/uploads/attachment_data/file/657842/ssac-occasional- paper-19-in-work-progression-and-universal-credit.pdf.

Stafford, B. *et al.* 2007. *New Deal for Disabled People: Third Synthesis Report – Key Findings from the Evaluation*. London: DWP. https:// www.researchgate.net/publication/308901136_New_Deal_for_ Disabled_People_Third_synthesis_report_-_key_findings_ from_the_evaluation.

Stewart, E. 2020. "What we know – and what we don't – about flexible working and productivity". In Carnegie/RSA (eds), *Can Good Work Solve the Productivity Puzzle?*

Strauss, D. 2021. "UK government position on labour market to fall vacant". *Financial Times*, 26 January. https://www.ft.com/content/ 4b5c4dbb-5638-4ff3-b9fb-ff7b8cf8dd10.

Sutherland, J. 2013. "Underemployment: a skills utilisation perspective". *Fraser Economic Commentary* 37(2): 76–86.

Taylor, G. 2021. "No space for Employment Bill in Queen's Speech". Lewis Silkin. https://www.lewissilkin.com/en/insights/no-space- for-employment-bill-in-queens-speech.

Taylor, M. 2017. *The Taylor Review of Modern Working Practices*. London: Department for Business, Energy and Industrial Strategy.

Timewise 2019. *The Timewise Flexible Jobs Index 2019*.

Timmins, N. 2016. *Universal Credit: From Disaster to Recovery?* London.

Trussell Trust 2021. "Trussell Trust data briefing on end-of-year statistics relating to use of food banks: April 2020–March 2021".

TUC 2020. *Disability Pay and Employment Gaps 2020*. London: TUC.

UK Parliament n.d.. Early Factory Legislation. https://www.parliament.uk/about/living-heritage/transformingsociety/livinglearning/19thcentury/overview/earlyfactorylegislation/.

Unison 2014. *Flexible Working: Making It Work*. https://www.unison.org.uk/content/uploads/2014/09/On-line-Catalogue225422.pdf.

Ussher, K. 2016. *Improving Pay, Progression and Productivity in the Retail Sector*. York: Joseph Rowntree Foundation.

Van Reenen, J. 2003. "Active labour market policies and the British new deal for the young unemployed in context". NBER Working Paper.

Walker, K. 1941. "The classical economists and the Factory Acts". *Journal of Economic History* 1(2): 168–77.

Wang S. *et al.* 2021. "Can active labour market programmes emulate the mental health benefits of regular paid employment? Longitudinal evidence from the United Kingdom". *Work, Employment and Society* 35(3): 545–65.

Warren, T. 2008. "Universal Disadvantage?" *European Societies* 10(5): 737–62.

Watts, B. *et al.* 2014. *Welfare Sanctions and Conditionality in the UK*. York: Joseph Rowntree Foundation.

Waugh, P. 2004. "Blair's reshuffle angers Brownites". *Evening Standard*, 8 September. https://www.standard.co.uk/hp/front/blair-s-reshuffle-angers-brownites-7233976.html.

Webster, D. 2018. *The Great Benefit Sanctions Drive 2010–16 in Historical Perspective*. Paper presented at the conference, Welfare Conditionality: Principles, Practices and Perspectives, York, June.

Whelan, N., M. Murphy & M. McGann 2021. "The enabling role of employment guidance in contemporary public employment services: a work-first to life-first typology". *British Journal of Guidance & Counselling* 49(2): 200–212.

Whitworth, A. & J. Griggs 2013. "Lone parents and welfare-to-work conditionality: necessary, just, effective?" *Ethics and Social Welfare* 7(2): 124–40.

Williams, E. 2021. "Punitive welfare reform and claimant mental health: the impact of benefit sanctions on anxiety and depression". *Social Policy & Administration* 55(1): 157–72.

Wishart, R. *et al.* 2019. *Changing Patterns in Parental Time Use in the UK*. London: NatCen.

Wolf, A. & K. Evans 2011. *Improving Literacy at Work*. London: Routledge.

Work and Pensions Committee 2018. "DWP's 'Clumsy and ill-judged attempt to piggyback' on IFS". https://committees.parliament.uk/committee/164/work-and-pensions-committee/news/97584/dwps-clumsy-and-illjudged-attempt-to-piggyback-on-ifs/.

Work and Pensions Committee 2021. *Disability Employment Gap*. https://publications.parliament.uk/pa/cm5802/cmselect/cmworpen/189/18902.htm.

Wright, S. & P. Dwyer 2021. "In-work Universal Credit: claimant experiences of conditionality mismatches and counterproductive benefit sanctions". *Journal of Social Policy* 51(1): 20–38.

Wright, S. *et al.* 2018. *Final Findings: Universal Credit*. Welfare Conditionality. http://www.welfareconditionality.ac.uk/wp-content/uploads/2018/05/40414-Universal-Credit-web.pdf.

Index